The apple Cookbook

The apple Cookbook

by Kyle D. Fulwiler

Pacific Search Press

Pacific Search Press, 222 Dexter Avenue North, Seattle, Washington 98109
© 1980 by Pacific Search Press. All rights reserved
Printed in the United States of America

Edited by Miriam Remak Bulmer
Cover illustration by Liz Gong

Library of Congress Cataloging in Publication Data
Fulwiler, Kyle D
  The apple cookbook.

  Includes index.
  1. Cookery (Apples) I. Title.
TX813.A6F84   641.6'4'11   79-12592
ISBN 0-914718-44-4

contents

Apples	7
Growing Apples	8
Choosing Apples	8
Storing Apples	9
Appetizers, Beverages, Preserves, and Sauces	15
Breakfasts, Brunches, and Breads	23
Sandwiches, Salads, Side Dishes, and Stuffings	37
Main Dishes	49
Desserts	61
Pies, Cookies, Cakes, Frostings, and Fillings	81
U.S. and Metric Measurements	103
Index	105

I want to express my gratitude to all the members of my extended family for their sincere help. Special thanks go to Gene and Orabell Avey, who were my most frequent tasters and critics, and to Betsy, who gave me an opportunity, then kept me going.

apples

Apples have long been a favored fruit. Adam and Eve succumbed to their voluptuousness. In Greek mythology, the tree bearing the Golden Apples of Hesperides was Earth's wedding gift to Hera and Zeus. Its highly prized fruits were guarded by a dragon that never slept. Today, the prudent scholar may be found polishing an apple for the teacher.

Although apples are now "as American as apple pie," and the United States produces more than any other nation in the world, the first primitive apples probably developed in Asia, very close to where modern Biblical scholars place the Garden of Eden. As civilization spread, so did these peripatetic fruits. The earliest annals of Egypt, Babylon, and China mention them, and fossilized apples have been found in Stone Age caves. The Greeks and Romans adopted them so completely that they tended to call any newly discovered fruit some type of apple — peaches were known as Persian apples, pomegranates were seed apples, and citrons were cedar apples. Later Europeans continued this custom, referring to tomatoes as love apples (*pommes d'amour*) and to potatoes as earth apples (*pommes de terre*).

By the fifteenth century, apples were an important crop in the Old World and the art of apple cultivation was fairly well advanced. Through selective propagation, the original small, sour Asian apple had become large, sweet, and juicy.

Apples, in the form of apple seeds, came to America with the first colonists. By 1750, apple orchards abounded and apple seeds were routinely tucked into every frontiersman's pack for the westward journey. One pioneer, John Chapman, spent most of his life establishing apple orchards in the newly settled American wilderness and became known and loved as Johnny Appleseed.

A major step in the apple's march west came in 1825, when a Hudson's Bay Company sailing vessel dropped anchor at Fort Vancouver, in what is now Washington State. On the banks of the Columbia River, the captain of the ship planted the seeds of an apple that had been given to him for luck at a farewell dinner in London. These seeds grew into the first apple trees in what is now the nation's top apple-producing state.

Since then, apples have spread from coast to coast and from border to border. They appear in pies, dumplings, and salads; they are turned into applesauce, apple cider, and apple butter. The American passion for apples has resulted in apple dishes ranging from simple (Apple Brown Betty) to sophisticated (Apples Valencia). Fortunately, through a combination of shipping and cold storage, you never need be without your apple a day. The only problem is deciding whether to eat it for breakfast (Apple Pancakes), lunch (Delicious Chicken Sandwiches), or dinner (Pork Chops with Apple Rings); as a dessert (Apple-Mint Mousse) or as a snack (Apple-Nutlettes). Kyle Fulwiler has made that decision even more difficult.

Growing Apples

Apples are members of the large and important rose family, Rosaceae. The kinship shows on both sides, for apple blossoms resemble miniature wild roses, while rose hips look like tiny apples.

Because they were grown from seeds, most early apples were of poor quality. When, out of the thousands planted, a seedling happened to produce good fruit, horticulturists propagated it by grafting its scions onto more vigorous, but less desirable, rootstocks. Today, grafted fruit trees are still the most successful and are available in any variety you care to grow.

Experts recommend having at least two different kinds of apple tree, for most apple trees require cross pollination. If space permits only one, a tree with two grafted varieties is the answer. Some nurseries even feature "three-graft" and "five-in-one" trees, with each grafted branch tagged. (Leave the tags on; a conscientious but forgetful gardener could eliminate one or more varieties at pruning time.)

Because climates vary, prospective apple growers should consult their local County Cooperative Extension Service office for information on which trees are most suitable for their area; advice on pruning, spraying, and fertilizing; and the best ways to prevent or cure apple scab, powdery mildew, and insect infestations.

Planting a tree is the easy part. Knowing what to do afterward determines the success of the venture.

Choosing Apples

Choosing the best apples for particular uses will help make your recipes successful. The chart on the following pages offers suggestions for using the apple varieties that are the most common and available of the hundreds now in existence.

Once you have chosen the kind of apple you want, check for appropriate color, texture, and size. Be sure each apple is free of brownish areas and that the color is good for that particular variety. On red apples, the background color should be slightly yellowish green. (Immaturity is indicated by a dark green color.) Check that each apple is firm, especially if it is large. If it is soft to the touch, it probably will be mealy and bland. Baking varieties are ideal when they are large.

Storing Apples

Whether you harvest them from your own trees, buy them from a fruit stand, or receive an unexpected windfall from a kind neighbor (or the wind), you may find that you have more apples than you can use immediately. Here are some suggestions to help make them last well into spring.

Home Storage

Ideally, apples should be kept in a highly humid atmosphere, and at close to freezing (31° to 32° Fahrenheit) without actually being frozen. While most homes do not have areas that meet these requirements, the crisper drawer in your refrigerator comes close. If you find this inconvenient or inadequate, the next best thing is a root cellar or a cold, damp basement. Experts disagree about whether the apples need to be wrapped and how they should be arranged. Some feel wrapping is unnecessary and the apples may be piled in several layers. Others recommend wrapping each apple in newspaper, then storing them in single layers, making sure they do not touch. (If you stack boxes of wrapped apples, be sure to leave space for air to circulate between each layer of boxes.) In either case, make sure you use only the most perfect apples available and sort through them often to discard any that show signs of spoiling. It is literally true that one bad apple can spoil a whole barrel.

Home stored apples should stay good for four to six months. If the apples lose their crispness, they may still be used for cooking, though they will be slightly harder to peel.

Freezing

There are two methods of freezing apples for later use. If the apples will be cooked after thawing, simply place the peeled, cored, and sliced apples in airtight one-quart containers, seal, and freeze. If they are to be used raw and their appearance is important, sprinkle

Variety	Main Season	Flavor & Texture
Cortland	Oct.–Jan.	Mild, tender
Red Delicious	Sept.–June	Sweet, mellow
Golden Delicious	Sept.–May	Sweet, semifirm
Granny Smith	Apr.–July	Tart, crisp
Gravenstein	July–Sept.	Tart, crisp
Jersey Red	Oct.–Apr.	Mild, firm
Jonathan	Sept.–Jan.	Tart, tender
McIntosh	Sept.–June	Slightly tart, tender
Newtown Pippin	Sept.–June	Slightly tart, firm
Rome Beauty	Oct.–June	Slightly tart, firm
Stayman	Oct.–Mar.	Tart, semifirm
Winesap	Oct.–June	Slightly tart, firm
Yellow Transparent	July–Aug.	Tart, soft
York Imperial	Oct.–Apr.	Tart, firm

Raw	Pie	Baking	Sauce	Freezing
Excel.	Excel.	Good	V. good	V. good
Excel.	Poor	Poor	Fair	Fair
Excel.	Excel.	V. good	V. good	V. good
V. good	V. good	V. good	V. good	V. good
Good	Good	Good	Good	Good
Good	V. good	Excel.	V. good	V. good
V. good	V. good	Poor	V. good	V. good
Excel.	Excel.	Fair	Good	Good
V. good	Excel.	V. good	Excel.	Excel.
Good	V. good	Excel.	V. good	V. good
V. good	Good	Good	Good	Good
Excel.	Good	Good	Good	V. good
Poor	Excel.	Poor	Good	Poor
Fair	Good	Good	V. good	Good

each quart of peeled, cored, and sliced apples with a combination of half a teaspoon of ascorbic acid or lemon juice, mixed into two tablespoons of water. Toss the fruit gently, seal in airtight one-quart containers, and freeze. Either way, try to use the apples within four months.

Applesauce may also be frozen for no more than four months, but make sure that when you pour it into the quart containers, you allow one inch headspace for expansion. You can also freeze your favorite pie filling; pour it into aluminum pie tins or into pie tins lined with foil. Wrap it with moisture-vapor proof freezer wrap and freeze. Later, you can place the frozen filling in a pie shell and add a top crust, or add just a top crust or a crumb topping; let the filling thaw and bake as usual.

Drying
Dried apples make excellent snacks and provide delicious nutrition in trail mixes or breakfast cereals. Reconstituted by an overnight soaking, they can be used in many cooked dishes when fresh apples are not available.

There are basically three methods of drying apples at home — sun drying, oven drying, and drying in a dehydrator — but before you use any of them, you must prepare the apples. Peel and core ripe, unbruised apples, then slice them into quarter-inch-thick rings or wedges. For faster drying, you may wish to make even thinner slices, or you may dice, chunk, or shred the apples. If you wish to keep the apples white as they dry, dip the pieces in pineapple juice, diluted lemon juice, or in a solution of one teaspoon ascorbic acid to one quart of water.

Sun drying is the most unreliable method because the weather can change unexpectedly, so use the thinnest possible slices or the smallest possible pieces to cut down on the drying time. Spread the apples over a screen or tray and cover with screening or netting (do not allow it to touch the fruit) to keep the insects off. Set the trays, either flat or at an angle, outside in the sun. Turn the apples occasionally until they are about two-thirds dry, then continue drying in the shade. Sun drying can take up to several days, depending on factors such as the warmth of the sun, the humidity in the atmosphere, and the thickness of the apples. If there is a chance of moisture at night, bring the apples in or cover and shelter them.

For oven drying, set your oven to the lowest possible setting and turn it on and off as needed to maintain a temperature between 95° and absolutely no more than 110° Fahrenheit (you might wish to invest in an oven thermometer for accurate readings). If you have a gas oven, the heat from the pilot light should be adequate. Just make sure that the temperature does not get too high or you will be cooking the apples, not drying them; this will cause loss of flavor, vitamins, minerals, and enzymes. Keep the oven door open for the best circulation. Place the apples on screens and set them on the oven racks, starting three inches from the bottom of the oven. Rotate the trays as needed for even drying and check for doneness by allowing a piece to cool before testing it. If the fruit shows signs of scorching, remove it immediately. The pieces of fruit should be done in six to twelve hours, depending on their thickness.

If you have a dehydrator, spread the apples in single layers and dry them according to the instructions. They will be done in twelve to eighteen hours, depending on the size of the slices and the type of dehydrator.

When the apples are dried to your taste, place them in small brown paper bags and fold the bags snugly around them. Place each paper bag in a similarly sized plastic bag and tightly fasten the plastic bag with a twist tab, or fold the top down and seal it with masking tape. For long-term storage, place one or more bags in two additional plastic bags or in a large airtight container. Sealed tightly, they should keep up to one year, depending on how much moisture was removed. Dried apples may also be stored in glass containers or in moisture-vapor proof polyethylene bags, but make sure they are *securely* sealed. Store in a cool, dark, dry place. Because dried apples can absorb moisture from the air, remember to check for mold about once a month.

Lucille Palmer, Pacific Search Press

appetizers, beverages, preserves, and sauces

Deviled Dip

Red apples 3
Lemon juice 2 teaspoons
Creamed cottage cheese 1 cup
Deviled ham 1 2¼-ounce can
Onion 1 teaspoon grated
Ripe olives 2 tablespoons chopped
Dry sherry 2 teaspoons

Cut apples into wedges, remove cores, and sprinkle with lemon juice. Combine remaining ingredients; pile into small bowl and surround with apple wedges. Makes 1½ cups of dip.

Pomme Fondue

Apples 2, cored and in chunks
Lemon juice 2 teaspoons
Sharp cheese spread 1 5-ounce jar
Milk 3 tablespoons

Brush apple chunks with lemon juice; set aside. Melt cheese spread in a heavy saucepan over low heat, then slowly blend in milk. Pour mixture into fondue pot and serve, using apple chunks for dunking. Serves 4.

Chicken Liver and Apple Kabobs

Apple juice ½ cup
Soy sauce 3 tablespoons
Cinnamon ¼ teaspoon
Cloves ⅛ teaspoon
Chicken livers ½ pound
Apple 1, cored, quartered, and in chunks
Bacon strips 12, halved

Mix together apple juice, soy sauce, cinnamon, and cloves; pour over chicken livers and marinate several hours. Cut livers into 2 or 3 pieces each. Wrap a piece of apple and a piece of liver in each bacon piece; secure with toothpicks. Arrange kabobs on a broiler rack and baste with marinade. Broil 4 inches from heat for 6 minutes, turning once. Bacon should be crisp and liver cooked. Makes 24 kabobs.

Spiced Apple Shake

Egg 1
Apple juice ¾ cup
Cinnamon ½ teaspoon
Milk ¼ cup
Ice cubes 2 (optional)

Combine all ingredients and mix in blender until well blended. Serves 1.

Hot Spiced Cider

Cinnamon sticks 6
Whole cloves 2 tablespoons
Coarsely filtered apple cider 1 gallon
Light brown sugar 1 cup

Tie spices in a piece of cloth and place in large saucepan with cider and sugar. Simmer covered for 20 minutes, then remove spice bag. Serve hot. Makes 1 gallon.

Wassail

Apple cider 6 cups
Cinnamon stick 1
Nutmeg ¼ teaspoon
Honey ¼ cup
Lemon peel 1 teaspoon grated
Lemon juice 3 tablespoons
Pineapple juice 1 18-ounce can
Butter 2 tablespoons
Orange 1, sliced into rings
Cinnamon sticks 1 per serving (optional)

In large saucepan, heat cider and cinnamon stick until boiling. Reduce heat, cover, and simmer 5 minutes. Stir in next 6 ingredients and simmer 5 minutes longer. Serve in punch bowl; float orange slices on top. Use cinnamon sticks as stirrers for each serving. Serves 16.

Hot Apple Nog

Apple cider 1 cup, hot
Sugar ½ cup
Salt ½ teaspoon
Cinnamon ¼ teaspoon
Nutmeg ⅛ teaspoon
Egg yolks 2
Milk 3 cups, hot
Egg whites 2
Whipping cream ½ cup, whipped until stiff

Combine first 6 ingredients in blender; blend until sugar is dissolved, then combine with milk. Beat egg whites until stiff and fold into milk mixture. Serve topped with whipped cream. Makes 8 ½-cup servings.

Apple Jelly

Apple juice   1 quart
Sugar   5 cups
Fruit pectin   1 1¾-ounce package
Water   ¾ cup

Place apple juice and sugar in a large bowl and set aside 10 minutes. Mix pectin with water; bring to a boil and boil 1 minute, stirring constantly. Stir pectin mixture into juice and continue stirring for 3 minutes. Pour into clean self-sealing jars or seal with paraffin, and leave at room temperature for 24 hours. May be stored indefinitely on a shelf. Makes 4 pints of jelly.

Pear and Apple Jam

Lemon   1
Sugar cubes   14
Pears   9, peeled and cored
Medium apples   7, peeled and cored
Sugar   5½ cups
Candied citrus peel   ¼ cup
Almonds   3 tablespoons chopped
Maraschino cherries   10, chopped

Remove zest from lemon by rubbing sugar cubes over lemon peel. Cut pears and apples into small pieces and place in large bowl. Squeeze lemon juice from lemon and pour juice over fruit. Cover fruit with sugar and sugar cubes; set aside overnight. Place fruit mixture in large kettle and add remaining ingredients. Over medium heat, cook, uncovered, for 1 hour or until soft, stirring occasionally. Liquefy in blender until roughly smooth, then return mixture to kettle and continue cooking until quite thick, about 20 minutes. Pour into jars and seal with paraffin. Makes 4 pints of jam.

Apple Butter

Apples   4 pounds, cored and quartered
Apple cider   2 cups
Brown sugar   2 cups
Cinnamon   1 teaspoon
Cloves   a dash

Cook apples and cider together in a large kettle over medium heat until very soft. Push mixture through strainer and return strained mixture to kettle, then add remaining ingredients. Cook over low heat, stirring constantly; make sure sugar dissolves. Continue cooking and stirring until mixture is very thick and coats the back of a spoon. Pour into hot, sterilized self-sealing jars. Makes 1½ pints of apple butter.

Apple Relish

Green peppers   3, halved and seeded
Apples   6, peeled and cored
Tomatoes   6
Onions   3
Celery   ½ cup diced
Raisins   2 cups
Cider vinegar   1 quart
Sugar   1½ cups
Salt   1 teaspoon

Force first 6 ingredients through a food chopper. Combine with remaining ingredients and cook over medium heat for 1 hour, or until thick and clear, stirring occasionally. Pour into sterile jars and seal. Makes 2 quarts of relish.

Apple-Raisin Chutney

Whole cloves   1 teaspoon
Raisins   1 pound, chopped
Nuts   ½ pound, chopped
Apples   4 pounds, peeled, cored, and chopped
Cider vinegar   3¾ cups
Sugar   4½ cups
Oranges   2
Sugar cubes   10

Tie cloves in piece of cloth. In large saucepan, combine raisins, nuts, apples, cloves, and 2½ cups of vinegar; cover and simmer until mixture is soft and thoroughly cooked, then remove cloves. Meanwhile, pour remaining 1¼ cups of vinegar over sugar and stir to dissolve. Remove zest from oranges by rubbing sugar cubes over the orange peels, then squeeze juice from oranges. Add vinegar-sugar mixture, orange juice, and sugar cubes to cooked fruit; cook, uncovered, until thick, stirring frequently to prevent burning and sticking. Pour into clean self-sealing jars; store until needed. Makes 3 quarts of chutney.

Applesauce

Apples   4, peeled, cored, and quartered
Water   1 cup
Brown sugar   ½ cup (optional)
Cinnamon   ⅛ teaspoon

Combine apples and water in a saucepan and bring to boiling. Reduce heat and simmer, stirring occasionally, until apples are quite soft. Mash apples and add brown sugar and cinnamon. Makes 4 cups of applesauce.

Sugarless Applesauce

Apple   1, peeled, cored, and chopped
Water   1 cup
Lemon juice   1 tablespoon
Cinnamon   2 dashes
Liquid artificial sweetener   1 tablespoon

Blend apple and water together in blender until smooth, then pour into saucepan. Add lemon juice and cinnamon, and boil until thick. Remove from heat and add artificial sweetener. Serves 1.

Spiced Pineapple-Raisin-Cider Sauce

Whole cloves   8
Cinnamon stick   1 2-inch piece
Brown sugar   ¼ cup
Cornstarch   1½ tablespoons
Salt   ⅛ teaspoon
Apple cider   1 cup
Raisins   ¼ cup
Pineapple chunks   ½ cup drained
Butter   1 tablespoon

Tie cloves and cinnamon stick in small piece of cloth and place in saucepan along with next 6 ingredients. Cook mixture over medium heat for 10 minutes, stirring constantly. Add butter, stir well, and remove spices. Makes 2 cups of sauce.
Note: This is excellent served with ham.

Cinnamon-Cider Sauce

Coarsely filtered apple cider   2 quarts
Large apples   6, peeled, cored, and quartered
Cinnamon   2 teaspoons

Place cider in large kettle and boil until reduced by ½. Cut apples lengthwise into ½-inch slices, add to cider, and simmer uncovered for 4 hours. Add cinnamon and allow to cool. Makes 1 quart of sauce.
Note: This is a delicious accompaniment to roasted meats.

breakfasts, brunches, and breads

Rise-and-Shine Cereal

Rolled oats   3 cups
Wheat germ   ½ cup
Sesame seeds   ¼ cup
Flaked coconut   1 cup
Salt   ½ teaspoon
Cashews   ½ cup
Sliced almonds   1 cup
Brown sugar   ⅓ cup
Vanilla   1 teaspoon
Dried apples   1 cup chopped
Raisins   1 cup

Mix together all ingredients except apples and raisins. Spread mixture in large baking pan and bake at 275° for 30 minutes. Stir well and add apples. Bake 30 minutes more, stirring every 10 minutes. Add raisins, cool, and store in covered container. Serve with milk or cream. Makes 8 cups of cereal.

Breakfast Puffs

Flour   2 cups
Sugar   1 tablespoon
Baking powder   1 tablespoon
Salt   ½ teaspoon
Cinnamon   ½ teaspoon
Eggs   2
Milk   1 cup
Vanilla   ½ teaspoon
Apples   1¼ cups peeled, cored, and diced
Oil or fat   for deep frying
Sugar   for coating

Sift together first 5 ingredients; set aside. Beat eggs until light, then add milk and vanilla. Blend in sifted ingredients, taking care not to overmix, then add apples. Heat oil to 375°. Drop batter in by teaspoonfuls and fry on both sides until golden brown. Drain and roll in sugar. Makes 3 dozen puffs.

Apple Pancakes

Pancake mix   enough for 8 pancakes,
   prepared according to directions on package
Apple   1, peeled, cored, and chopped
Cinnamon   2 teaspoons

Stir all ingredients together and cook as directed for ordinary pancakes. Serves 2 to 3.

German Pancake

Eggs   4
Flour   ½ cup
Baking powder   ½ teaspoon
Sugar   1 tablespoon
Salt   a pinch
Milk   1 cup
Vanilla   1 teaspoon
Margarine   2 tablespoons, melted
Apple Topping

Put first 7 ingredients in blender and blend until smooth; set aside 30 minutes. Brush a 10-inch ovenproof skillet with margarine, pour in batter, and bake at 425° for 15 minutes. Reduce temperature to 375° and bake 10 minutes longer. Spread pancake with Apple Topping and cut into wedges to serve. Serves 3.

Apple Topping

Apple   1, peeled, cored, and grated
Lemon juice   2 teaspoons
Honey   1 tablespoon
Cream cheese   1 3-ounce package, softened

Combine all ingredients thoroughly.

Apple Roll-Ups

Cream cheese   2 3-ounce packages
Brown sugar   ¼ cup
Honey   ¼ cup
Apple   ⅓ cup peeled and finely chopped
Nuts   ¼ cup chopped
Refrigerated crescent rolls   2 8-ounce packages
Margarine   2 tablespoons
Honey   2 tablespoons
Nuts   2 tablespoons finely chopped

Mix together cream cheese, brown sugar, and honey; add apple and nuts. Separate crescent rolls into triangles. Put 1 tablespoon of mixture on the wide part of each triangle, spread over dough, and roll up. Place rolls point side down on an ungreased cookie sheet; pinch ends together to make a ring. Bake at 350° for 18 to 20 minutes. Mix together remaining ingredients; spread over each roll while still warm. Makes 16 rolls.

Quick Apple Roll-Ups

Sugar   ⅓ cup
Cinnamon   ½ teaspoon
Refrigerated crescent rolls   1 8-ounce package
Apple   1, peeled, cored, and in eighths
Margarine   3 tablespoons, melted

Mix together sugar and cinnamon. Separate crescent dough into 8 pieces. Dip each apple slice in margarine, then coat with cinnamon mixture. Place each slice on a piece of dough and wrap up, pinching all edges together. Brush rolls with remaining margarine and bake at 350° for 18 to 22 minutes. Makes 8 rolls.

Sweet Rolls with Apple

Apples   1¼ cups peeled, cored, and chopped
Sugar   ½ cup
Raisins   ¼ cup
Cinnamon   ¼ teaspoon
Ginger   a dash
Nutmeg   ⅛ teaspoon
Orange juice   1 tablespoon
Refrigerated crescent rolls   1 8-ounce package
Butter   1 tablespoon, melted

In small bowl, combine first 7 ingredients. Separate crescent rolls and form dough into 2 large rectangles, then overlap long sides to make a 7 by 13-inch rectangle; press dough together firmly along seam. Brush with melted butter and spread with apple mixture. Roll up jelly roll style, starting with short end. Cut into 8 slices and place, cut sides down, in greased muffin tins. Bake at 350° for 25 to 30 minutes. Makes 8 rolls.

Apple-Cheddar Brunch Dumplings

Apples   2, peeled, cored, and chopped
Cheddar cheese   1 cup grated
Sugar   ½ cup
Walnuts   ½ cup coarsely chopped
Flour   2 tablespoons
Cinnamon   2 teaspoons
Nutmeg   ⅛ teaspoon
Refrigerated crescent rolls   2 8-ounce packages

Combine first 7 ingredients and stir well. Separate crescent rolls into 8 rectangles, pressing seams together; cut each rectangle in ½. Place 2 tablespoons of apple mixture on each square, then seal each square by pulling the 4 corners together and twisting top. Bake at 375° for 12 to 15 minutes, or until golden brown. Serve warm. Makes 16 dumplings.

Apple Brunchies

English muffins 2, split
Apple 1, peeled, cored, and in 20 slices
Margarine 2 tablespoons, melted
Brown sugar ¼ cup
Cinnamon to taste

Place muffin halves on a cookie sheet, split sides up. Put 5 apple slices on each, brush with melted margarine, and sprinkle with brown sugar and cinnamon. Bake at 425° for 15 minutes, or until apples are tender. Serves 4.

Apple Blintzes

Ricotta cheese 1 cup
Sugar ¼ cup
Vanilla 1 teaspoon
Lemon peel ½ teaspoon grated
Salt ½ teaspoon
Apples 2, peeled, cored, and grated
Dessert Crepes (see Index) 14, warm
Butter 2 tablespoons, melted
Sugar to taste

Combine first 5 ingredients and beat well, then stir in apples. Fill each crepe with 1 tablespoon of filling and roll up. Arrange blintzes on warm ovenproof serving platter and brush each with melted butter. Bake at 300° for 10 minutes; sprinkle with sugar before serving. Makes 14 blintzes.

Apple-Filled Brunch Cake

Flour 1¼ cups
Sugar ¾ cup
Salt 1 teaspoon
Baking powder 1 teaspoon
Cinnamon ½ teaspoon
Nutmeg ⅛ teaspoon
Vanilla ½ teaspoon
Margarine ⅓ cup
Milk ⅓ cup
Eggs 2
Apple 1, peeled, cored, and very thinly sliced
Sugar 2 tablespoons
Cinnamon ½ teaspoon
Flour ⅓ cup
Brown sugar ⅓ cup
Margarine 3 tablespoons
Pecans ⅓ cup chopped

Combine first 10 ingredients in mixing bowl and blend with electric mixer on low speed until all ingredients are moistened. Increase speed to medium and beat 2 minutes. Spread ½ of batter in a greased 9 by 9-inch pan; arrange apple slices over batter. Combine remaining 2 tablespoons of sugar and ½ teaspoon of cinnamon, and sprinkle over apples; spoon remaining batter over all. Combine remaining ingredients and sprinkle over batter. Bake at 350° for 30 minutes.

Coffee Cake with Apple Streusel Topping

Flour   1½ cups
Baking powder   1 tablespoon
Sugar   ½ cup
Salt   ¼ teaspoon
Butter   ¼ cup
Egg   1
Milk   ½ cup
Apple   ½ cup peeled, cored, and finely chopped
Brown sugar   ½ cup
Cinnamon   2 teaspoons
Flour   2 tablespoons
Butter   2 tablespoons, melted
Nuts   ½ cup chopped

Sift flour, baking powder, sugar, and salt together. Cut in butter with fork or pastry blender. Beat egg and milk together, and add to mixture. Spread ½ the batter in a greased and floured 6 by 10-inch pan. Mix together remaining ingredients; spread ½ this mixture over batter, then repeat layers. Bake at 375° for 25 to 30 minutes.

Apple Bread

Butter or margarine   ½ cup
Sugar   1 cup
Eggs   2
Unsweetened chocolate   ½ ounce, melted
Flour   1½ cups
Salt   ½ teaspoon
Cloves   ½ teaspoon
Cinnamon   1 teaspoon
Baking soda   1 teaspoon
Strong coffee   ½ cup, cold
Apples   1 cup cored and chopped
Raisins   ½ cup
Walnuts   ½ cup chopped

Combine butter, sugar, eggs, and chocolate; beat until light and creamy. Sift together flour, salt, and spices. Dissolve baking soda in coffee. Alternately mix flour and coffee mixtures into butter mixture. Stir in apples, then add raisins and nuts. Spoon batter into greased and floured 5 by 9-inch loaf pan; bake at 350° for 45 to 50 minutes. Cool in pan for 10 minutes before turning out onto cake rack.

Hearty Wheat Bread

Flour   1½ cups
Salt   ½ teaspoon
Baking soda   1 teaspoon
Whole wheat flour   1½ cups
Margarine   ¼ cup
Sugar   ½ cup
Egg   1
Apple   ¾ cup peeled, cored, and grated
Prune juice   ¼ cup
Buttermilk   1 cup
Walnuts   1 cup broken

Sift together flour, salt, and baking soda; stir in whole wheat flour and set aside. In large bowl, cream together margarine and sugar. Beat in egg, then add apple and prune juice. Alternately add buttermilk and sifted ingredients to creamed mixture; mix well and fold in walnuts. Pour batter into a greased 5 by 9-inch loaf pan and bake at 350° for 1¼ hours. Cool before removing from pan.

Applesauce Loaf

Margarine ½ cup
Sugar 1 cup
Eggs 2
Flour 1¾ cups
Baking powder 1 teaspoon
Salt 1 teaspoon
Baking soda ½ teaspoon
Cinnamon ½ teaspoon
Applesauce 1 cup
Walnuts ½ cup chopped

Cream together margarine and sugar, then beat in eggs, 1 at a time. Sift together next 5 ingredients and add to creamed mixture alternately with applesauce. Stir in walnuts, then pour batter into greased 5 by 9-inch loaf pan. Bake at 350° for 1 hour. Cool before removing from pan.

Apple Butter Bread

Flour 1½ cups
Baking powder 2 teaspoons
Sugar ½ cup
Cinnamon 1 teaspoon
Nutmeg ¼ teaspoon
Salt ¼ teaspoon
Egg 1
Margarine ¼ cup, melted
Apple butter ½ cup
Milk ¼ cup
Apple cider ¼ cup
Walnuts ½ cup chopped
Flour 2 tablespoons

Sift first 6 ingredients into a large bowl and make a well in the center. Place next 5 ingredients in well and mix with large spoon just until all ingredients are moistened. Mix nuts with 2 tablespoons flour and fold into mixture. Pour batter into a well-buttered 5 by 9-inch loaf pan and set aside 15 minutes before baking at 350° for 45 minutes. Cool before removing from pan.

Apple-Cheddar Bread

Flour   2 cups
Baking powder   1 teaspoon
Baking soda   ½ teaspoon
Salt   ½ teaspoon
Margarine   ½ cup
Sugar   ⅔ cup
Cheddar cheese   ½ cup grated
Eggs   2, slightly beaten
Apples   1½ cups peeled, cored, and shredded
Chives   1 tablespoon chopped
Nuts   ½ cup chopped

Sift together flour, baking powder, soda, and salt; set aside. Cream together margarine and sugar, then add cheese and mix until smooth. Stir in eggs and mix well. Alternately add apples and sifted ingredients, ½ at a time, mixing well after each addition. Stir in chives and nuts, then pour batter into a greased 5 by 9-inch loaf pan. Bake at 350° for 50 to 60 minutes. Cool before removing from pan.

Z. Appleseed Bread

Flour   2 cups
Cinnamon   1 tablespoon
Baking soda   2 teaspoons
Salt   1 teaspoon
Baking powder   ¼ teaspoon
Eggs   3
Sugar   1 cup
Brown sugar   1 cup
Oil   1 cup
Vanilla   1 tablespoon
Zucchini   1 cup coarsely grated and loosely packed
Apples   1 cup peeled, cored, and grated
Raisins   1 cup

Sift together first 5 ingredients and set aside. Beat eggs until frothy, then add sugar, brown sugar, oil, and vanilla; continue beating until thick. Stir in zucchini, apples, and sifted ingredients; fold in raisins. Pour batter into 2 greased 5 by 9-inch loaf pans and bake at 350° for 1 hour, or until done. Cool before removing from pans. Makes 2 loaves.

Plum-Apple Loaf

Apples   2 cups peeled, cored, and finely chopped
Sugar   1 cup
Egg   1
Margarine   ½ cup, melted
Orange peel   2 tablespoons grated or
    Dried orange peel   2 tablespoons
Flour   1½ cups
Baking soda   1 teaspoon
Salt   ½ teaspoon
Cinnamon   1 teaspoon
Canned plums   ½ cup chopped
Raisins   ½ cup
Nuts   ½ cup chopped

Combine apples and sugar; set aside 10 minutes. Add egg and mix well, then stir in margarine and orange peel. Sift together flour, baking soda, salt, and cinnamon; add to apple mixture and mix well for 2 minutes. Add remaining ingredients, then pour batter into 2 greased 3 by 7-inch loaf pans. Bake at 350° for 55 minutes. Cool before removing from pans. Makes 2 loaves.

Apple-Pumpkin Bread

Flour   2 cups
Baking powder   2 teaspoons
Baking soda   ½ teaspoon
Salt   1 teaspoon
Cinnamon   1 teaspoon
Nutmeg   ½ teaspoon
Canned pumpkin   1 cup
Sugar   1 cup
Milk   ½ cup
Eggs   2
Margarine   ¼ cup, softened
Apples   1 cup peeled, cored, and grated

Sift together first 6 ingredients; set aside. Combine next 5 ingredients in large bowl and mix well. Add sifted mixture, then stir in apples. Pour batter into a greased 5 by 9-inch loaf pan and bake at 350° for 50 minutes, or until a toothpick inserted in center comes out clean. Cool before removing from pan.

Johnnycake Surprise

Apple   1, peeled, cored, and thinly sliced
Raisins   ¼ cup
Brown sugar   3 tablespoons
Corn muffin mix   1 8½-ounce package,
      prepared according to directions on package

Arrange apple slices evenly over bottom of an 8 by 8-inch baking pan and sprinkle with raisins and brown sugar. Pour corn muffin batter evenly into pan and bake at time and temperature recommended on package. Cut into squares and serve warm. Serves 8.

Apple Crowns

Flour   2 cups, sifted
Brown sugar   ¼ cup
Baking powder   1 tablespoon
Salt   ¾ teaspoon
Apple   1, peeled, cored, and grated
Egg   1, beaten
Milk   ¾ cup
Oil   ¼ cup
Brown sugar   3 tablespoons
Cinnamon   1 teaspoon
Nutmeg   1 teaspoon
Apples   1 cup peeled, cored, and in thin wedges

Sift together flour, brown sugar, baking powder, and salt; add grated apple. Combine egg, milk, and oil, and add to flour mixture, stirring just until dry ingredients are moistened. Fill paper-lined muffin tins ⅔ full of batter. Combine brown sugar and spices; coat remaining apples with mixture. Press apple wedges into batter, core edge first, to make stripes; be sure to press firmly or they will pop up during cooking. Bake at 400° for 20 to 25 minutes. Makes 12 muffins.

Apple Gems

Apple 1, peeled, cored, and shredded
Rolled oats 1½ cups
Oil ¼ cup
Salt ½ teaspoon
Raisins ½ cup
Walnuts ½ cup chopped
Egg 1

Combine all ingredients thoroughly and set aside 10 minutes. Fill oiled muffin tins ½ full, pressing batter down firmly. Bake at 375° for 25 minutes. Makes 12 gems.

Nutty Apple Muffins

Flour 2 cups
Sugar ½ cup plus 2 tablespoons
Salt ¾ teaspoon
Baking powder 1 tablespoon
Cinnamon ½ teaspoon
Cloves a dash
Nutmeg ¼ teaspoon
Margarine ½ cup
Egg 1
Milk 1 cup
Apples 1 cup peeled, cored, and grated
Walnuts or pecans 1 cup chopped

Sift together first 7 ingredients. Cream margarine and add egg, then slowly beat in milk. Add sifted ingredients; stir until smooth. Add apples and nuts, mixing well. Fill well-greased muffin tins ⅔ full and bake at 375° for 30 minutes. Makes 12 muffins.

sandwiches, salads, side dishes, and stuffings

Delicious Chicken Sandwiches

Apple 1, cored and shredded
Chicken 1 cup cooked and diced
Slivered almonds ¼ cup, toasted
Mayonnaise ⅓ cup
Bread slices 8, buttered to taste

Mix together apple, chicken, almonds, and mayonnaise; spread mixture on ½ the bread slices and cover with remaining slices. Makes 4 sandwiches.

Creamy Herring Sandwiches

Herring snacks 1 12-ounce jar
Apple 1, peeled, cored, and shredded
Onion ½ cup finely chopped
Celery ¼ cup finely chopped
Dillweed 1 teaspoon
Dijon mustard 1 tablespoon
Sour cream ½ cup
Mayonnaise for spreading (optional)
Bread slices 8

Chop herring into ¼-inch cubes and combine with apple, onion, celery, and dillweed. Stir in mustard and sour cream, then chill several hours. Spread mayonnaise on bread slices, then spread filling on ½ the slices and cover with remaining slices. Makes 4 sandwiches.

Waldorf Salad

Apples 2, cored and chopped
Celery 1 cup diced
Raisins ½ cup
Walnuts ⅓ cup coarsely chopped
Mayonnaise ½ cup
Lettuce leaves (optional)

Toss together apples, celery, raisins, and walnuts; stir in mayonnaise. Serve in 1 large bowl or on individual, lettuce-lined plates. Serves 4 to 6.

Marinated Mushroom Salad

Mushrooms   1 pound, thinly sliced
Olive oil   ½ cup
Lemon juice   ½ cup
Cream   2 tablespoons
Medium onion   1, thinly sliced
Large apple   1, peeled, cored, and thinly sliced
Watercress   2 bunches

Marinate mushrooms in oil, lemon juice, and cream for 1 hour. Combine with remaining ingredients, toss, and serve. Serves 6.

American Apple Salad

Celery stalks   2
Ice water
Apples   4
Cream   3 tablespoons
Lemon juice   1 tablespoon
Sugar   1 teaspoon
Salt   a pinch
Walnut halves   4

Shred celery very finely and place in bowl of ice water. Wipe and polish apples with a soft cloth. Cut off bottoms and carefully scoop out the pulp. Discard cores and seeds, then chop pulp. Drain and dry shredded celery, add to chopped apple, and mix well; place in bowl. Blend together cream, lemon juice, sugar, and salt; pour over apple-celery mixture and stir carefully until fruit is well coated. Spoon mixture into apple shells and decorate each apple with a walnut half. Serves 4.

Christmas Salad

Jellied cranberry sauce ½ 1-pound can
Sour cream ½ cup
Apples 2 cups cored and chopped
Walnuts 1 cup chopped
Celery 1 cup sliced
Lettuce leaves 6

Mash cranberry sauce with fork and blend in sour cream. Stir in apples, walnuts, and celery. Mound onto lettuce leaves and serve. Serves 6.

Apple-Sauerkraut Salad

Sauerkraut 1 27-ounce can, undrained
Sugar ⅓ cup
Small red onion 1, thinly sliced
Apple 1, cored and diced
Celery ½ cup thinly sliced
Celery seeds ¼ teaspoon

Combine all ingredients in a large bowl; chill well. Serves 8.
Note: This will keep up to 8 weeks in the refrigerator.

Ham and Apple Slaw

Cabbage 3 cups shredded
Ham 1½ cups shredded
Apples 2, peeled, cored, and cubed
Mayonnaise ⅓ cup
Vinegar 2 to 3 tablespoons

Combine all ingredients and serve immediately. Serves 6.

Curried Chicken Salad

Chicken   3 cups cooked and cubed
Celery   1 cup thinly sliced
Apple   1, cored and diced
Pineapple chunks   1 20-ounce can, drained
Seedless grapes   1 cup
Sliced almonds   ¼ cup
Mayonnaise   1 cup
Catsup   1 tablespoon
Curry powder   1½ teaspoons
Lettuce leaves

Combine first 6 ingredients. Mix together mayonnaise, catsup, and curry powder; toss well with chicken mixture. Serve on small, lettuce-lined plates. Serves 8.

Scandinavian Shrimp Salad

Raisins   1 cup
Boiling water
Apples   1 cup peeled, cored, and chopped
Eggs   2, hard-cooked and chopped
Shrimp   2 cups
Celery   ½ cup chopped
Potatoes   2, cooked, peeled, and diced
Onion   1 tablespoon minced
Green pepper   ½ cup diced
Mayonnaise   1 cup
Whipped topping   1 cup
Lemon juice   2 teaspoons

Place raisins in a strainer and dip in boiling water for 1 minute; drain and combine with next 7 ingredients. Thoroughly mix remaining ingredients and combine with salad mixture. Refrigerate overnight before serving. Serves 12.

Molded Apple-Cheese Salad

Lemon-flavored gelatin   1 3-ounce package
Boiling water   1½ cups
Cottage cheese   1 cup
Lemon juice   2 tablespoons
Crushed pineapple   1 8½-ounce can, drained
Red apples   2 cups cored and chopped
Walnuts   ½ cup chopped

Dissolve gelatin in boiling water; cool slightly. Blend cottage cheese in blender until smooth, then pour into bowl and add remaining ingredients. Stir mixture into cooled gelatin, blend well, and pour into a 4-cup mold or into a 9 by 13-inch glass dish. Refrigerate until set. Serves 6 to 8.

Ginger Ale Salad

Lemon-flavored gelatin   1 3-ounce package
Boiling water   1 cup
Ginger ale   1 cup
Apples   1 cup peeled, cored, and chopped
Nuts   ¼ cup finely chopped
Celery   ¼ cup finely chopped
Lettuce leaves   6
Mayonnaise   6 tablespoons

Dissolve gelatin in boiling water. Add ginger ale and chill until mixture begins to thicken, then fold in apples, nuts, and celery. Pour into 8 by 8-inch pan and chill until set. Cut into 6 squares and place each square on a lettuce leaf; dot each with 1 tablespoon of mayonnaise. Serves 6.

Molded Apple Cream

Unflavored gelatin 1 tablespoon
Apple juice 4 cups
Cream cheese 1 8-ounce package

In a small saucepan, soften gelatin in ½ cup apple juice. Soften cream cheese by beating with an electric mixer. Heat softened gelatin until just boiling, then add to remaining apple juice. Beat mixture into cream cheese, pour into a 4-cup mold, and chill until set. Serves 8.

Spiced Apples

Whole cloves 2 tablespoons
Cinnamon sticks 5
Whole allspice 1 teaspoon
Sugar 8 cups
Salt 1 teaspoon
Cider vinegar 2½ cups
Small apples 3 pounds peeled and cored*

Tie spices in a piece of cloth and place in saucepan with sugar, salt, and vinegar; bring to a boil. Add apples and cook uncovered over medium heat for 20 minutes, or until tender, turning frequently. Remove apples with a slotted spoon and place in wide-mouth jars. Remove spice bag and boil syrup for 5 minutes, or until thick; add to apples. This will keep up to 1 month in refrigerator. Makes 1 quart.
* Make sure you weigh the apples *after* they've been peeled and cored.

Minted Apples

Sugar 1 cup
Water ½ cup
Green food coloring 3 drops
Mint flavoring 5 drops
Small apples 4, peeled, cored, and halved

Boil sugar and water together for 5 minutes; stir in food coloring and mint flavoring. Add apples to syrup, cover tightly, and simmer slowly until apples are tender. Remove with slotted spoon and cool before using. Serves as garnish for 8.
Note: This is very good with roast turkey or leg of lamb.

Poached Apples

Water 1 cup
Sugar ¼ cup
Apples 2, peeled, cored, and halved

Combine water and sugar in an 8-inch frying pan. Cook over low heat until sugar dissolves. Add apples, round side down. Heat to simmering and cook for 15 to 20 minutes or until tender. Baste occasionally with syrup from pan. Remove from syrup with a slotted spoon. Serves as garnish for 4.
Variations: Add one of these flavorings to syrup — dried lemon peel, cinnamon sticks, vanilla, or liqueurs.
Note: Serve as a garnish, dressed up with mint jelly or cranberry sauce in the middle. Chilled with yogurt or sour cream, poached apples also make a delicious accompaniment to a meal.

Fried Apples

Butter 1 tablespoon
Apples 2, cored and cut crosswise into ¼-inch slices

Heat butter in a frying pan until foaming. Reduce heat to medium and fry for 1 minute on each side. Do not overcook or rings will fall apart. Serves 4 as a garnish.
Variations: Sprinkle with a thin layer of sugar (white or brown) before turning, or sprinkle with cinnamon just before removing from pan, or flame with 2 tablespoons brandy before serving.
Note: Serve with pancakes, French toast, or as a garnish for roasted meats.

Apple Stir Fry

Onion 1, sliced
Oil 1 tablespoon
Apples 2, peeled, cored, and in chunks
Sugar 2 teaspoons
Lemon juice to taste
Salt and pepper to taste

In skillet or wok, sauté onion in oil for 10 minutes, or until golden brown. Add apples, sugar, and lemon juice; cover and steam until apples are slightly soft. Season and serve. Serves 4.

Glazed Apple Bake

Apples 5, peeled, cored, and sliced
Lemon peel of 1 lemon, grated
Lemon juice of 1 lemon
Cloves 1/8 teaspoon
Brown sugar 1 cup
Cinnamon 1/2 teaspoon
Water 1 1/2 cups
Brown sugar 1 cup

Arrange slices in 8 by 8-inch baking dish. Place next 6 ingredients in medium bowl; mix well and pour over apples. Bake at 375° for 25 minutes, then sprinkle with remaining cup of brown sugar and broil until sugar begins to caramelize. Serve warm with roasted fowl. Serves 8.

Baked Apple Relish Cups

Apples 6
Margarine 2 tablespoons
Onions 1 cup finely chopped
Tomato 1, peeled and chopped
Raisins 1/4 cup
Preserved ginger 1 tablespoon finely chopped
Dried, crushed red pepper 1/4 teaspoon
Dry mustard 1/4 teaspoon
Green pepper 1/4 cup finely chopped
Red currant jelly 1/4 cup
Vinegar 1/4 cup

Slice off apple bottoms and remove insides with a small spoon or grapefruit knife. Discard seeds and chop apple pulp. Melt margarine in a skillet; add onions and sauté until soft. Stir in next 6 ingredients, plus chopped apple and 1 tablespoon each of jelly and vinegar. Cook over moderate heat for 5 minutes, stirring occasionally. Spoon mixture into apple shells and arrange apples in 9 by 13-inch baking dish. Combine remaining jelly and vinegar in a small saucepan and heat until jelly melts; spoon sauce over and around apples. Bake at 350° for 25 minutes, then cool 15 minutes and baste with pan juices before serving. Serves 6.
Note: This is very nice with meat loaf.

Red Cabbage Casserole

Medium red cabbage   1, quartered, cored, and finely shredded
Boiling water   to cover cabbage
Onion   1, sliced
Margarine   2 tablespoons
Apples   2, peeled, cored, and sliced
Wine vinegar   3 tablespoons
Water   3 tablespoons, plus as needed
Sugar   ¾ tablespoon
Brown sugar   ¾ tablespoon
Salt and pepper   to taste
Margarine   2 tablespoons
Flour   1 tablespoon

Blanch cabbage in boiling water for 1 minute, then drain. Over medium high heat, cook onion and margarine in large ovenproof pan until onion is soft. Add apples and cook several minutes more, then place in bowl. Alternate layers of cabbage and apple-onion mixture in pan and sprinkle with next 5 ingredients. Cover tightly and bake at 325° for 1½ hours, or until tender, stirring occasionally and moistening with extra water if necessary. Meanwhile, cream together remaining margarine and flour. Slowly add to casserole after baking, in order to bind. Serves 8.
Note: This is excellent with wild game.

Noodles and Apples

Sugar   ¼ cup
Cinnamon   ½ teaspoon
Cloves   ¼ teaspoon
Nutmeg   a dash
Wide noodles   4 cups cooked
Apples   4 cups peeled, cored, and sliced
Butter   2 tablespoons

Combine sugar and spices. Place ¼ of noodles in a buttered 2-quart casserole. Alternate layers of ⅓ sugar mixture, ⅓ apples, and ¼ noodles, ending with noodles; dot each layer of noodles with butter. Cover dish and bake at 375° for 45 minutes; uncover and bake 15 minutes longer. Serves 6.

Apple-Prune Stuffing

Onion   1 tablespoon minced
Shortening   2 tablespoons, melted
Very small, dried bread cubes   1 cup
Apples   2 cups cored and finely chopped
Chicken stock   ½ cup
Salt and pepper   to taste
Prunes   ½ cup, cooked and drained

Brown onion in shortening over medium high heat; add bread cubes and apples. Mix in just enough chicken stock to moisten mixture, season to taste, and add prunes. Makes enough to stuff a 3½-pound chicken or duck.

Apple and Raisin Stuffing

Onions   1 cup minced
Apples   3 cups peeled, cored, and diced
Raisins   1 cup
Salt   1½ teaspoons
Pepper   ⅛ teaspoon
Dried bread cubes   7 cups
Sugar   ¼ cup
Margarine   ¾ cup, melted

Combine all ingredients and mix well. Makes enough to stuff a 10-pound turkey.

main dishes

Apple and Beef Ragout

Beef drippings or oil   1½ tablespoons
Chuck steak   1½ pounds, in 1½-inch cubes
Onions   4, in 1-inch cubes
Carrots   4, peeled, quartered, and in 1½-inch pieces
Flour   1½ tablespoons
Beef stock   2½ cups
Garlic clove   1, crushed
Tomato puree   1 teaspoon
Salt and pepper   to taste
Parsley sprigs   2
Bay leaf   1
Thyme   ½ teaspoon
Apples   3, peeled, cored, and quartered

Heat ovenproof 4-quart casserole and add drippings. Add beef and brown well over medium high heat. Remove beef and reduce heat to medium. Add onions and carrots; cook until they begin to color, then add flour and cook several minutes longer. Add stock, garlic, tomato puree, seasonings, and beef. Tie parsley and bay leaf together; add to casserole along with thyme. Bake at 350° for 1½ hours, then add apples and cook 15 minutes more. Remove parsley and bay leaf, and serve. Serves 4.

Meat Loaf with Apples

Ground beef   1 pound
Dry bread crumbs   ¾ cup
Egg   1, beaten
Onion   3 tablespoons finely chopped
Salt   ¾ teaspoon
Dry mustard   ¼ teaspoon
Pepper   ¼ teaspoon
Garlic salt   ¼ teaspoon
Worcestershire sauce   2 teaspoons
Apples   2, peeled, cored, and thinly sliced

Thoroughly combine all ingredients except apples. Press ½ of mixture into a greased 5 by 9-inch loaf pan. Press apple slices into meat and cover with remaining meat. Bake at 350° for 1½ hours. Serves 6.

Liver and Apples

Calf's liver 1½ pounds
Butter ½ cup
Apples 6, peeled, cored, and in sixths
Sugar ¼ cup
Vinegar 1 teaspoon
Salt 1½ teaspoons
Black pepper ½ teaspoon
Chicken broth ¼ cup
Apple juice 1 cup
Cornstarch 1½ tablespoons
Lemon juice 1 tablespoon
Currant jelly 2 tablespoons

Rinse liver, cut in narrow strips, and pat dry; set aside. Melt ½ the butter in a skillet; add apples, sprinkle with sugar, and cook over low heat for 8 minutes, turning frequently. Melt remaining butter in another skillet and sauté liver for 3 minutes. Add vinegar, seasonings, and broth; cook 3 minutes more. In small saucepan, combine 2 tablespoons of apple juice with cornstarch; add remaining ingredients and remaining apple juice, and cook over low heat until thick. Arrange apples in a serving dish, arrange liver over them, and moisten with several spoonfuls of sauce. Serve remaining sauce separately. Serves 6.

Stuffed Veal Birds

Flour ⅓ cup
Salt 1 teaspoon
Pepper ¼ teaspoon
Celery salt ¼ teaspoon
Veal round steak 1 to 1½ pounds, boned and quartered
Soft bread cubes ½ cup
Celery ¼ cup chopped
Small apple 1, peeled, cored, and chopped
Mustard ¼ teaspoon
Sherry 1 tablespoon
Oil 2 tablespoons
Chicken bouillon cube 1
Hot water 1 cup, plus as needed

Combine flour, salt, pepper, and celery salt; pound mixture into veal with a mallet until mixture is gone. Combine next 5 ingredients; mix well. Place ¼ of stuffing on each piece of veal and roll up; fasten with string. Heat oil in skillet and brown meat well. Dissolve bouillon cube in water; add to skillet, cover, and simmer for 1½ hours, adding extra water if necessary. Serves 4.

Apple-Stuffed Crown Roast of Pork

Crown roast of pork 7 pounds or 16 ribs
Salt 1 teaspoon
Pepper ¼ teaspoon
Chicken bouillon cubes 2
Hot water ½ cup
Medium onions 3, chopped
Celery ½ cup sliced
Margarine 6 tablespoons
Apples 3 cups peeled, cored, and finely chopped
Dried bread cubes 3 cups
Parsley ¼ cup chopped
Thyme ½ teaspoon
Nutmeg ¼ teaspoon
Honey 2 tablespoons
Apple juice 2 tablespoons

Place roast, rib ends up, in a shallow roasting pan. Mix together salt and pepper, and rub over roast. Insert a meat thermometer, making sure it doesn't touch a bone, and bake at 325° for 1½ hours. In the meantime, dissolve bouillon cubes in hot water; set aside. Cook onions and celery in margarine over medium heat until soft. Stir in apples and continue cooking for 3 minutes, then remove from heat. In large bowl, combine onion mixture with bread cubes, parsley, thyme, nutmeg, and chicken bouillon; toss until evenly moistened. Remove roast from oven and stuff center, mounding slightly. Loosely cover stuffing with foil and bake another 1½ hours; baste with mixture of honey and apple juice during last 15 minutes. To serve, carve into individual chops. Serves 10 to 12.

Stuffed Pork Chops

Pork chops   6, 1 inch thick
Celery   ¼ cup
Raisins   ¼ cup
Apple   1, peeled, cored, and chopped
Soft bread crumbs   1 cup
Salt   1 teaspoon
Butter   1 tablespoon, melted
Oil   for browning
Water   as needed

Cut a lengthwise pocket in each chop. Mix together next 6 ingredients and stuff chops; if mixture falls out, sew up with large needle and string. Brown chops in a little oil, then bake at 350° for 1 hour, adding a little water during cooking to prevent dryness. Serves 6.

Smothered Pork Chops

Pork chops 6, ¾ inch thick
Salt ¼ teaspoon
Oil 2 tablespoons
Apples 3, peeled, cored, and in ½-inch slices
Molasses 3 tablespoons
Flour 3 tablespoons
Hot water 2 cups
Cider vinegar 1 tablespoon
Salt ½ teaspoon
Yellow raisins ⅓ cup

Sprinkle chops with ¼ teaspoon salt and brown slowly in oil in hot skillet; reserve fat drippings. Place chops in large shallow baking dish; arrange apples over chops and cover with molasses. Stir flour into fat in skillet and cook until brown; gradually stir in hot water and heat to boiling. Stir in remaining ingredients and pour sauce over chops and apples. Cover and bake at 350° for 1 hour. Serves 6.

Pork Chops with Apple Rings

Flour ¼ cup
Salt a dash
Pepper a dash
Pork chops 4
Oil for frying
Butter 3 tablespoons
Apples 2, peeled, cored, and in thick rings
Brown sugar 2 tablespoons

Mix together flour, salt, and pepper. Coat pork chops with flour mixture and fry in hot oil for 10 minutes, or until golden brown; keep warm. Heat butter in skillet until sizzling and fry apple rings over medium heat until golden brown. Add brown sugar and cook until dissolved. Place pork chops in serving dish, cover with apples, and serve. Serves 4.

Pork Chop Stew

Shoulder pork chops   6
Onions   3, thinly sliced
Carrots   3, peeled, quartered, and in 1½-inch pieces
Apples   4, peeled, cored, and sliced
Brown sugar   4 teaspoons
Salt and pepper   to taste

Trim fat from chops and cut fat into thin strips; set aside. Layer ½ the onions, carrots, and apples in a 4-quart casserole; sprinkle with ½ the brown sugar. Add single layer of chops, then layer remaining onions, carrots, and apples, plus pork fat over chops. Sprinkle with remaining brown sugar plus seasonings, cover, and bake at 350° for 1½ hours. Serves 3 to 6.

Ham-Apple Casserole

Ham   3½ cups ground
Onion   1 tablespoon minced
Soft bread crumbs   1 cup
Cloves   ¼ teaspoon
Mustard   ½ teaspoon
Egg   1, beaten
Milk   ½ cup
Salt   to taste
Apples   3, peeled, cored, and sliced
Honey   ¼ cup
Butter or margarine   2 tablespoons

Mix together first 8 ingredients and pack into shallow 8 by 11-inch baking dish. Arrange apples over mixture, dribble with honey, and dot with butter. Cover and bake in preheated 375° oven for 40 minutes. Serves 4 to 6.

Sausages and Apples

Apples 2, cored and sliced
Brown sugar 3 tablespoons
Long-grain rice 1 cup, cooked
Link sausages (not precooked) ½ pound
Catsup ¼ cup

Arrange apples in bottom of a greased 2-quart casserole; sprinkle with brown sugar. Layer rice over apples, then arrange sausages over rice; cover with catsup. Cover and bake at 350° for 30 to 45 minutes, then uncover and bake 15 minutes more. Serves 4.
Note: The sausages will be less greasy if you cover them with boiling water, set them aside 3 minutes, and drain, before adding to casserole.

Apple–Sweet Potato Casserole with Sausages

Sweet potatoes 4 cups thinly sliced
Apples 4 cups thinly sliced
Onion 2 tablespoons minced
Salt 2 teaspoons
Maple syrup ½ cup
Apple cider 1 cup
Margarine ½ cup, melted
Brown-and-serve sausages 12

Arrange sweet potatoes and apples in alternate layers in a greased 2-quart casserole, sprinkling each layer with onion and salt. Combine syrup, cider, and margarine; pour over casserole. Cover and bake 1 hour at 350°. Arrange sausages on top and bake uncovered for 20 minutes more. Serves 6.

Frankfurter-Apple Bake

Frankfurters 1½ pounds
Onion 1, chopped
Apples 2, peeled, cored, and sliced
Brown sugar 1 tablespoon
Tomato juice 1 cup

Broil frankfurters on rack; drain on paper towels and slice into 1-inch pieces. Arrange frankfurters, onion, and apples in 1½-quart casserole. Combine brown sugar and tomato juice; pour over casserole. Bake at 350° for 1 hour. Serves 4.

Lamb and Apple Stew with Biscuits

Lamb 1 pound boneless, cubed
Flour 2 tablespoons
Oil 2 tablespoons
Water 2 cups
Bay leaf 1
Salt 1 teaspoon
Parsley 1 teaspoon chopped
Thyme ½ teaspoon
Pepper ⅛ teaspoon
Onion 1, in ½-inch slices
Apples 3 cups peeled, cored, and sliced
Water 1 cup
Sugar 3 tablespoons
Refrigerated biscuits 1 8-ounce package

Coat lamb with flour, then fry in hot oil until well browned. Place lamb in large ovenproof casserole and add next 7 ingredients. Cover and cook at 350° for 1½ to 2 hours, or until tender, stirring occasionally. Remove onion and bay leaf. Add apples, 1 cup water, and sugar; bake 15 to 20 minutes more. Top with biscuits, and bake at 425° for 12 to 15 minutes. Serves 4 to 6.
Note: You may turn the stew into a clean 1½-quart casserole before topping with biscuits for a nicer table presentation.

Baked Chicken with Apples

Chicken   3 pounds, in pieces
Salt and pepper   to taste
Nutmeg   to taste
Oil   2 tablespoons
Apple juice   ¼ cup
Lemon juice   2 teaspoons
Honey   2 tablespoons
Apple juice   ¾ cup
Lemon juice   1 tablespoon
Apple   1, peeled, cored, and finely chopped
Apples   2, cored and in eighths

Sprinkle chicken with salt, pepper, and nutmeg. Spread oil in a 9 by 13-inch baking pan; arrange chicken pieces in pan. Combine ¼ cup apple juice with 2 teaspoons lemon juice; pour over chicken. Bake at 375° for 40 minutes, basting occasionally. In a small saucepan, combine honey with remaining apple juice and lemon juice. Bring to a boil and add finely chopped apple; boil 5 minutes, or until sauce begins to thicken, then add sliced apples. Arrange baked chicken on serving platter. Strain pan juices into sauce, stir sauce, and spoon over chicken. Serves 4 to 6.

Sweet-and-Sour Chicken

Oil   1 tablespoon
Chicken breasts   2, boned and in 1-inch cubes
Pineapple   1 20-ounce can
Brown sugar   ¼ cup
Cornstarch   2 tablespoons
Vinegar   ¼ cup
Soy sauce   2 tablespoons
Small green pepper   1, in squares
Onion   ½, thinly sliced
Apples   1 cup peeled, cored, and chopped
Small tomato   1, in chunks
Rice   6 servings

Heat oil in large skillet or wok, add chicken, and cook over medium high heat (350° in electric appliance) 5 minutes, or until tender. Drain pineapple, reserving syrup, and cut pineapple into chunks; set aside. Combine pineapple syrup with brown sugar, cornstarch, vinegar, and soy sauce, mixing well. Lower heat to medium (300°); add syrup mixture to chicken and cook just until it begins to thicken. Add pineapple chunks plus green pepper, onion, apples, and tomato; cook until just heated through, making sure not to overcook. Serve over hot rice. Serves 4.

desserts

Easy Apples

Brown sugar ¼ cup
Cinnamon ½ teaspoon
Nutmeg ½ teaspoon
Small apples 6, peeled and cored
Flour ⅔ cup
Sugar ⅔ cup
Baking powder ¼ teaspoon
Salt ⅛ teaspoon
Egg 1, slightly beaten
Margarine 3 tablespoons, melted
Vanilla 1 teaspoon

Mix together brown sugar, cinnamon, and nutmeg. Roll each apple in mixture and place in individual buttered custard cups. Sprinkle each apple with remaining mixture and set aside. Sift together flour, sugar, baking powder, and salt. Combine egg, margarine, and vanilla; add to dry ingredients. Spoon 2 tablespoons of this batter over each apple. Place cups on a cookie sheet (in case they boil over) and bake at 375° for 40 to 45 minutes. Serves 6.

Baked Apples

Apples 4, cored
Sugar 4 tablespoons

Place apples in a greased 8 by 8-inch ovenproof baking dish. Bake until soft, but not mushy (about 30 minutes) at 375°. Serves 4.
Variations: Omit sugar and fill with the equivalent of 1 tablespoon brown sugar substitute per apple, or add chopped nuts, raisins, candied fruit, or mincemeat to centers while baking.
Note: Serve chilled baked apples with ice cream or with a dollop of whipped cream on top.

Baked Apples with Cranberry Sauce

Apples   4, cored
Whole cranberry sauce   1½ cups
Sugar   ¼ cup
Orange peel   of 1 orange, grated

Place apples in a baking dish; fill centers with cranberry sauce and pour remaining sauce around apples. Mix together sugar and orange peel; sprinkle mixture over apples. Bake at 350° for 40 minutes, basting frequently. Serves 4.

Orange Apples

Sugar   3 cups
Water   3 cups
Apples   6, cored
Orange juice   of 2 oranges
Orange peel   of 2 oranges, grated
Whipped cream   topping (optional)

Boil together sugar and water for 1 minute. Add apples, cover, and cook gently until tender. Remove apples carefully and place in a serving dish. Add orange juice and peel to syrup and simmer uncovered for 20 minutes, or until liquid is reduced to 2 cups. Pour ½ the syrup over apples and refrigerate 1 hour. Cover with remaining syrup and serve with whipped cream. Serves 6.

Stuffed Meringue Apples

Sugar   5 tablespoons
Water   2 cups
Vanilla   ¼ teaspoon
Large apples   6, peeled and cored
Mixed dried fruit   ¾ cup chopped
Butter   2 tablespoons
Egg whites   2
Sugar   ½ cup
Chocolate sauce   1 4-ounce can, hot

Bring sugar and water to a boil; add vanilla and boil slowly for 10 minutes, or until slightly thick. Poach apples in syrup for 15 minutes, or until tender, turning occasionally. Remove from pan with a slotted spoon and arrange in 9 by 13-inch baking dish or in individual baking dishes; set aside. In a small saucepan, mix dried fruit with butter and 1½ tablespoons of syrup. Stir over gentle heat for 5 minutes, then stuff each apple with this mixture. Whip egg whites until stiff, then whisk in 1 tablespoon of sugar and whisk 1 minute; fold in remaining sugar until well mixed. Using a spoon or a piping bag with a rose tip, cover each apple with meringue. Bake at 275° for 15 to 20 minutes, or until golden brown. Pour hot chocolate sauce around apples and serve. Serves 6.

Candied Fruit and Apple Bake

Apples   1 to 1½ pounds, peeled, cored, and sliced
Brown sugar   to taste
Nutmeg   ½ teaspoon
Lemon peel   of 1 lemon, grated
Lemon   1, peeled and segmented
Candied fruit   5 tablespoons
Boiling water
Butter   1 tablespoon
Bread slices   4, buttered and crusts removed
Egg whites   2
Sugar   5 tablespoons, plus a sprinkle

Arrange apples in buttered 6-inch soufflé dish or in 8-inch pie tin, layering with brown sugar, nutmeg, lemon peel, and lemon segments. Plunge candied fruit into boiling water for 1 minute, then drain and arrange over apples. Spread butter over a butter wrapper and cover fruit with wrapper. Bake at 375° for 30 minutes, or until apples are soft. Remove wrapper and cover dish with bread slices. Return to oven until bread browns. Whip egg whites until stiff and whisk in 2 teaspoons of sugar; continue whisking 1 minute, then carefully fold in remaining sugar. Pile meringue over dish, sprinkle with sugar, and brown lightly at 300°. Serves 6.

Apples Valencia

Medium sugar cubes   25
Water   ½ cup
Oranges   2 to 3
Boiling water
Sugar   ¾ cup
Water   2 cups
Apples   4 to 5, peeled, cored, and quartered

Dissolve sugar cubes in ½ cup water; boil rapidly until rich brown, about 5 minutes. Pour caramel onto an oiled cookie sheet and allow to set until hard, then crush into fairly small pieces; set aside. Pare rind from ½ an orange and cut it into fine shreds. Simmer shreds in 2 inches of boiling water for 5 to 6 minutes, then drain and rinse with cold water. Remove peels and pith from remaining oranges; slice oranges into thin rounds and set aside. Place sugar and 2 cups of water in saucepan and dissolve sugar over gentle heat, then boil rapidly for 1 minute. Add apples to syrup at once, cover, and simmer 10 to 15 minutes, or until tender. Remove saucepan from heat and leave covered until cold, then carefully lift apples into a glass bowl. Arrange orange rounds on top, and spoon a little syrup over all. Sprinkle with crushed caramel and shredded orange rind; chill and serve. Serves 4.

Apple Pudding

Flour ¾ cup
Sugar ½ cup
Baking powder 1 teaspoon
Salt ¼ teaspoon
Apples 1½ cups peeled, cored, and coarsely chopped
Almonds ½ cup
Milk ½ cup
Brown sugar ¾ cup
Margarine ¼ cup
Boiling water ¾ cup

Sift together flour, sugar, baking powder, and salt. Add apples, almonds, and milk; mix well and spread in a well-greased 1½-quart casserole. Combine remaining ingredients; stir until margarine is melted. Pour over apple mixture and bake at 375° for 40 to 50 minutes. Serves 8.

Baked Apple-Graham Pudding

Medium apples 4, peeled, cored, and sliced
Brown sugar ½ cup
Graham cracker crumbs 1 cup
Water ¾ cup
Lemon juice 3 tablespoons
Nutmeg 1 teaspoon
Cream topping

Combine first 6 ingredients and mix well. Place in well-greased 12 by 12-inch baking dish and bake at 375° for 30 minutes. Serve hot with fresh cream. Serves 4.

Wonderful Rice Pudding

Rice 1 cup, cooked and cooled
Sugar ⅓ cup
Crushed pineapple 1 13½-ounce can, drained
Vanilla ½ teaspoon
Miniature marshmallows ⅓ cup
Red apples 1 cup cored and chopped
Whipping cream 1 cup, whipped until stiff

Mix together rice, sugar, pineapple, and vanilla. Stir in marshmallows and apples. Fold in whipped cream. Serves 4 to 6.

Apple Tapioca

Quick-cooking tapioca ¼ cup
Boiling water 2 cups
Salt ¼ teaspoon
Apples 4, peeled, cored, and quartered
Sugar ½ cup
Cinnamon ¼ teaspoon (optional)
Butter 1 tablespoon
Cream or whipped cream topping

In the top of a double boiler, combine tapioca, boiling water, and salt; cook until clear. Place apples in a buttered 1½-quart casserole and sprinkle with sugar and cinnamon. Dot with butter, cover with cooked tapioca, and bake at 350° for 35 minutes, or until apples are tender. Serve hot with cream. Serves 6.

Apple Tapioca Ambrosia

Sugar ½ cup
Quick-cooking tapioca ¼ cup
Salt a dash
Apple juice 2½ cups
Apples 1 cup peeled, cored, and chopped
Oranges 2, peeled and in chunks
Flaked coconut ¼ cup

Combine sugar, tapioca, salt, and apple juice in saucepan; let stand 5 minutes, then cook over medium heat until mixture boils, stirring constantly. Pour into medium-sized serving bowl, cool slightly, and stir in apples and oranges. Chill at least 1 hour. Sprinkle with coconut just before serving. Serves 6.

Apple-Mint Mousse

Sugar ½ cup
Cinnamon 1 teaspoon
Mace ⅛ teaspoon
Applesauce 2 cups
Lemon juice 1 tablespoon
Peppermint extract ½ teaspoon
Green food coloring 2 to 3 drops
Whipping cream 1 cup

Combine sugar, cinnamon, and mace; add to applesauce and stir until sugar dissolves. Add lemon juice, peppermint extract, and food coloring. Whip cream and fold into applesauce mixture. Spoon into ice trays and freeze at least 2 hours, or until firm. Serves 6.

Apple Parfait

Applesauce 2 cups
Sugar 2 tablespoons
Cinnamon 1 teaspoon
Lemon juice 1 teaspoon
Nutmeg ¼ teaspoon
Vanilla ice cream 1 quart
Almonds ¼ cup chopped, toasted

Combine first 5 ingredients in saucepan and cook over moderate heat for 5 minutes. Cool, then layer into 6 individual parfait glasses with vanilla ice cream. Top with almonds and serve immediately. Serves 6.

Applesauce Soufflé

Eggs 4
Applesauce 1¼ cups
Sugar 1 cup
Cinnamon ¼ teaspoon
Whipping cream 1 cup
Unflavored gelatin 2 tablespoons
Water 5 tablespoons
Whipping cream ¼ cup, whipped until stiff

Wrap a piece of waxed paper around a 6-inch soufflé dish so it rises 4 inches above the dish. Separate eggs, placing whites in 1 bowl and yolks in another. Add applesauce, sugar, and cinnamon to yolks, place bowl over pan of hot water, and beat with electric mixer for 5 minutes, or until very thick. Whip cream until partially stiff and fold into yolk mixture. Over gentle heat, dissolve gelatin in water; stir into yolk mixture. Place bowl over ice and stir until mixture begins to thicken. Beat egg whites until stiff, but not dry; fold into yolk mixture. Pour into prepared soufflé dish and chill 1 hour or until set. Remove paper collar and decorate with remaining whipped cream. Serves 4 to 6.

Kitchen Cobbler

Flour 1 cup
Salt ½ teaspoon
Baking soda ½ teaspoon
Brown sugar ½ cup
Rolled oats 1 cup
Margarine ½ cup
Applesauce 1 20-ounce can
Butter 2 tablespoons

Sift together flour, salt, baking soda, and brown sugar; combine with oats, then cut in margarine until crumbly. Spread ½ of mixture in greased 9-inch pie tin. Cover with applesauce, dot with butter, and cover with remaining mixture. Bake at 350° for 40 to 45 minutes. Serves 6.

Apple Peanut Crisp

Apples 6, peeled, cored, and thinly sliced
Brown sugar ½ cup
Flour 3 tablespoons
Cinnamon 1 teaspoon
Nutmeg ½ teaspoon
Salt ¼ teaspoon
Flour 1 cup
Brown sugar ¼ cup
Peanut butter ½ cup
Margarine ¼ cup
Cream cheese 1 3-ounce package

Arrange apples in a buttered 9 by 13-inch baking dish. Combine next 5 ingredients and spread over apples. Combine remaining ingredients, mixing with a fork until mixture looks crumbly. Spread over apples and bake at 400° for 25 minutes. Serves 8.

Apple Sesame Crisp

Apples 5, peeled, cored, and sliced
Cinnamon 1 teaspoon
Nutmeg ¼ teaspoon
Lemon juice 1 teaspoon
Brown sugar ½ cup
Sugar ½ cup
Flour ¾ cup
Butter or margarine ½ cup
Sesame seeds 3 tablespoons

Arrange apples in a buttered 9 by 13-inch baking dish; sprinkle with spices and lemon juice. Mix sugars and flour, then cut in butter until mixture resembles bread crumbs. Add sesame seeds and spread mixture over apples. Bake at 375° for 1 hour. Serves 8.

Healthy Apple Crisp

Rolled oats ¾ cup
Flour ¾ cup
Brown sugar ½ cup
Wheat germ ¼ cup
Nuts ¼ cup chopped
Salt ¼ teaspoon
Margarine ¼ cup
Large apples 6, peeled, cored, and sliced
Raisins ½ cup

Combine first 6 ingredients, then cut in margarine until mixture forms crumbs the size of small peas. Arrange apples in a buttered 9 by 11-inch baking dish; cover with raisins. Sprinkle crumbly mixture over all and press down gently. Bake at 350° for 30 minutes. Serves 8 to 10.

Apple Brown Betty

Margarine ⅓ cup, melted
Soft bread crumbs* 2 cups
Apples 2 pounds, peeled, cored, and sliced
Brown sugar ½ cup
Nutmeg ½ teaspoon
Cinnamon ¼ teaspoon
Lemon juice 2 tablespoons
Water ¼ cup
Vanilla Sauce (see Index) or cream topping

Toss margarine with bread crumbs; arrange ⅓ of crumbs in a greased 1½-quart casserole. Arrange ½ the apples over the crumbs. Combine brown sugar, nutmeg, and cinnamon; sprinkle ½ over apples. Repeat layers and cover with remaining crumbs. Pour lemon juice and water over all, cover, and bake at 375° for 30 minutes. Uncover and bake 30 minutes more. Serve warm with Vanilla Sauce. Serves 6.
*Soft bread crumbs may be made by putting torn up slices of bread into the blender and blending.

Apple-Cinnamon Crepes with Vanilla Sauce

Sugar 1 cup
Water 2 cups
Apples 8, peeled, cored, and quartered
Brown sugar 1 cup
Lemon peel 1 teaspoon grated or
　　Dried lemon peel 1 teaspoon
Water 1½ cups
Butter 1 tablespoon
Cornstarch 1 tablespoon
Lemon juice 2 tablespoons
Salt a dash
Cinnamon 1½ tablespoons
Dessert Crepes 14 to 16
Vanilla Sauce
Slivered almonds ¼ cup, toasted

Combine sugar and water in saucepan; cook over gentle heat until sugar dissolves. Poach apples in sugar syrup for 15 minutes, or until tender. Strain, cut apples into smaller slices, and set aside. Combine brown sugar, lemon peel, water, and butter; heat to boiling. Mix cornstarch with lemon juice and add to mixture. Add salt, cinnamon, and apples; heat to boiling. Fill each crepe with apple filling and arrange on large serving dish or on individual dishes. Cover with enough Vanilla Sauce to moisten and sprinkle with almonds. Serve additional Vanilla Sauce separately. Makes 14 to 16 filled crepes.

Dessert Crepes

Flour 1½ cups
Sugar 1 tablespoon
Baking powder ½ teaspoon
Salt ½ teaspoon
Milk 2 cups
Eggs 2
Vanilla ½ teaspoon
Butter 2 tablespoons, melted
Butter 2 tablespoons

Sift together flour, sugar, baking powder, and salt. Pour milk, eggs, and vanilla into a blender and mix well. Slowly add dry ingredients and blend until smooth, then add 2 tablespoons of melted butter and mix until blended. Allow batter to stand 30 minutes before using. To make crepes, heat remaining 2 tablespoons of butter in shallow 6-inch cast iron or aluminum skillet and swirl it around. When butter is completely melted and sizzling, wipe out pan with paper towel. Pour in about 2 tablespoons of batter and swirl this around until the bottom of the pan is covered. (Good crepes should be lacy looking, not thick like pancakes.) When batter is set, turn and cook other side. Continue until all the batter is used up. Makes 14 to 16 6-inch crepes.

Vanilla Sauce

Milk 1¼ cups
Vanilla 1 tablespoon
Egg yolks 3
Sugar 3 tablespoons
Arrowroot 1 teaspoon

Scald milk with vanilla. Cream egg yolks with sugar and arrowroot. Add milk to creamed mixture and stir until well mixed. Return mixture to saucepan and stir continuously over gentle heat until mixture coats the back of a wooden spoon. Strain into a bowl and allow to cool. Makes 1½ cups of sauce.

Apple Crepe Cake with Apricot Sauce

Butter   1 tablespoon
Apples   1½ to 2 pounds, peeled, cored, and sliced
Lemon peel   to taste, grated or
   Dried lemon peel   to taste
Sugar   to taste
Cinnamon   to taste
Dessert Crepes (see Index)   14 to 16
Apricot Sauce

Rub butter over the bottom of a heavy saucepan; add apples, lemon peel, sugar, and cinnamon. Cover and cook slowly until tender. Arrange crepes in an 8 by 8-inch baking dish or a 9-inch pie tin, alternating with apple mixture. Bake at 350° for 10 minutes. Cut "cake" into 8 portions and pour a little Apricot Sauce over the top and around the portions. Serve remaining sauce separately. Serves 8.

Apricot Sauce

Apricot jam   6 tablespoons
Lemon juice   of 1 lemon
Lemon peel   of 1 lemon, grated
Water   1¼ cups
Arrowroot   1½ teaspoons
Water   1 to 2 tablespoons

Place jam, lemon juice, lemon peel, and water in saucepan; heat gently until jam dissolves. Mix arrowroot with remaining water, add to saucepan, and heat to boiling, stirring constantly. Cook 2 to 3 minutes, or until sauce clears, then strain. Makes 1½ cups of sauce.

Bourdelots

Apples 6, peeled and cored
Lemon juice 1 tablespoon
Powdered sugar 3 tablespoons
Cinnamon 1 teaspoon
Nutmeg ¼ teaspoon
Rich Shortcrust Pastry (see Index)
    enough for 1 double-crust pie, chilled
Walnuts ¼ cup chopped
Egg yolk 1
Water 1 tablespoon
Sour cream 1 cup

Brush apples with lemon juice. Mix powdered sugar, cinnamon, and nutmeg together; roll each apple in mixture. Roll out pastry into a large rectangle and cut into 6 equal squares. Place 1 apple on each square. Divide walnuts equally and stuff apples. Wrap pastry around each apple and pinch seams together. Mix egg yolk with water; brush onto pastry. Place bourdelots in a greased 9 by 13-inch baking dish; bake at 400° for 45 minutes. Top each with sour cream and serve. Serves 6.

Apple Dumplings

Apples 4
Water 2 cups
Sugar ½ cup
Shortcrust Pastry (see Index) enough for 1 double-crust pie, chilled or
  Piecrust sticks 2, prepared according to directions on package, chilled
Cinnamon 2 teaspoons
Sugar ½ cup
Cream topping (optional)

Peel and core apples, reserving peels. Thinly slice apples and set aside. Place peels in a saucepan with water and ½ cup sugar; bring to a boil, then simmer 20 minutes, then strain. Meanwhile, roll out piecrust mix into a rectangle and cut it into 6 5-inch squares. Divide apple slices evenly and arrange on each square. Sprinkle squares with cinnamon and remaining ½ cup sugar. Seal each square around apples by pinching pastry together. Place dumplings in a deep buttered baking dish. Pour enough apple peel liquid into dish to cover dumplings halfway. Bake at 425° for 40 minutes, basting once. Serve warm with fresh cream. Serves 6.

Rosy Dumplings

Sugar ¾ cup
Water ¾ cup
Cinnamon ⅛ teaspoon
Nutmeg ⅛ teaspoon
Red food coloring 2 drops
Margarine 2 tablespoons
Flour 1½ cups
Baking powder 1½ teaspoons
Salt ½ teaspoon
Shortening ½ cup
Milk ⅓ cup
Apples 4, peeled and cored
Brown sugar ½ cup
Margarine 2 tablespoons

Combine first 5 ingredients in saucepan and bring to a boil. Stir in margarine and set aside. Sift together flour, baking powder, and salt. Cut in shortening, add milk, and toss until a ball of dough forms. Turn dough onto floured board and knead about 10 times. Roll out to ¼-inch thickness and cut into 4 6-inch squares. Place an apple in the center of each square; sprinkle apples with brown sugar and dot with remaining margarine. Draw corners of pastry together and seal edges. Place in greased 9 by 13-inch baking dish, leaving an inch between dumplings. Pour syrup over all and bake at 375° for 40 minutes. Serves 4.

Apple Squares

Flour   2½ cups
Sugar   1 tablespoon
Salt   1 teaspoon
Lard or shortening   1 cup
Egg yolk   1
Milk   ¼ cup
Cornflakes   2 cups crushed
Apples   3, peeled, cored, and sliced
Sugar   1 cup
Cinnamon   1 teaspoon
Nutmeg   ½ teaspoon
Egg white   1
Powdered sugar   1 cup
Milk

Mix together flour, sugar, and salt; cut in lard. Mix in egg yolk and milk, and chill well. Turn ½ of dough onto a floured board and roll into a large enough rectangle to line the bottom and sides of a 6 by 10-inch baking pan. Spread 1 cup of cornflakes evenly over pastry; arrange apple slices over cornflakes, sprinkle with sugar, cinnamon, and nutmeg, and spread remaining cornflakes over apples. Roll out remaining pastry and fit to cover pan. Beat egg white until fluffy and spread over top crust. Bake at 400° for 35 to 45 minutes. Cool slightly and drizzle with mixture of powdered sugar and enough milk to make a thin frosting. Cut into squares and serve. Serves 8.

Sour Cream Apple Squares

Margarine ½ cup
Yellow cake mix 1 18½-ounce package
Apples 2, peeled, cored, and thinly sliced
Sour cream 1 cup
Egg 1
Brown sugar ¼ cup
Cinnamon ½ teaspoon
Nutmeg ¼ teaspoon
Almonds ¼ cup chopped and toasted

Cut margarine into cake mix until crumbly; set aside ⅔ cup. Press remaining cake mixture into the bottom of a buttered 9 by 13-inch pan and arrange apples on top. Blend sour cream with egg and spread over the apples. Combine reserved cake mixture with remaining ingredients and sprinkle over sour cream. Bake at 350° for 25 to 30 minutes, or until golden brown and bubbly. Serve warm. Serves 10.

Lois's Apple Torten

Flour 2 cups, sifted
Egg yolks 2
Sugar ½ cup
Lemon peel of 1 lemon, grated
Salt ¼ teaspoon
Margarine ¾ cup
Apples 6, peeled, cored, and sliced
Sugar ¾ cup
Cinnamon 1 teaspoon
Margarine 2 tablespoons
Egg yolks 2
Cream 6 tablespoons

Place first 6 ingredients in bowl and work together until well blended. Press dough into a 1 by 7 by 11-inch baking pan, covering bottom and sides. Lay apples in rows over dough, sprinkle with sugar and cinnamon, and dot with margarine. Cover with foil and bake for 15 minutes at 350°. Beat remaining egg yolks with cream, pour over apples, and bake uncovered for 30 to 40 minutes, or until crust is golden brown. Serves 10 to 12.

Cinnamon-Apple Pinwheels

Sugar   1½ cups
Water   1½ cups
Red cinnamon candies   ¼ cup
Flour   2 cups
Sugar   ¼ cup
Baking powder   2 teaspoons
Salt   ½ teaspoon
Butter   ⅓ cup
Egg   1
Milk   to equal ⅔ cup when combined with egg
Butter   1 tablespoon, softened
Apples   3 cups peeled, cored, and chopped
Cinnamon   ½ teaspoon
Whipped cream   topping (optional)

Combine sugar, water, and cinnamon candies in a saucepan; bring to a boil and simmer 5 minutes. Set aside ½ cup of mixture and pour remainder into an 8 by 12-inch baking pan. Sift together flour, sugar, baking powder, and salt; cut in ⅓ cup butter. Beat together egg and milk with fork, then add to flour mixture and mix well. Turn dough onto a floured board and knead about 12 times, then roll out into a 12-inch square. Spread with softened butter, cover with apples, and sprinkle with cinnamon. Roll up like a jelly roll, cut into 1½-inch slices, and place slices in pan with syrup, cut sides down. Bake at 400° for 30 minutes, then spoon reserved syrup over each pinwheel and bake 10 to 15 minutes longer. Serve with whipped cream. Serves 8.

Autumn Apple Bake

Refrigerated biscuits   1 8-ounce package
Apples   2, peeled, cored, and thinly sliced
Brown sugar   ½ cup
Milk   ½ cup
Cinnamon   ½ teaspoon
Dark corn syrup   ½ cup
Margarine   ¼ cup

Separate biscuits and arrange them in the bottom of a greased 8 by 8-inch pan; arrange apples over biscuits. Combine remaining ingredients in a saucepan; heat to boiling, stirring constantly. Pour hot syrup over biscuits and bake at 375° for 20 to 25 minutes, or until golden brown. Serve warm. Serves 6 to 8.

Caramel Apples

Caramels   1 14-ounce package
Water   2 tablespoons
Wooden skewers   5
Apples   5

In double boiler over low heat, melt caramels with water, stirring occasionally until smooth. Put skewers into stem ends of apples and dip each apple into hot caramel, turning until well coated. Place on greased waxed paper and chill until firm. Makes 5 caramel apples.

Apple-Nutlettes

Unflavored gelatin   2½ tablespoons
Applesauce   1¼ cups
Sugar   2 cups
Walnuts   1 cup chopped
Vanilla   2 teaspoons
Powdered sugar   to coat

Stir gelatin into ½ cup applesauce; set aside. In saucepan, combine remaining applesauce with sugar and bring to a boil. Add gelatin mixture and simmer 15 minutes, then add nuts and vanilla. Pour mixture into buttered 8 by 8-inch pan and let set until cool. Cut into cubes and sprinkle with powdered sugar. Makes 3 dozen candies.

pies, cookies, cakes, frostings, and fillings

Apple Pie

Shortcrust Pastry   for 8-inch double-crust pie
Apples   5 cups peeled, cored, and thinly sliced
Sugar   ½ cup
Flour   3 tablespoons
Cinnamon   ¼ teaspoon
Salt   a pinch
Margarine   1 tablespoon

Roll out ½ of pastry and line 8-inch pie tin. Spread apples over pastry. Combine sugar, flour, cinnamon, and salt; sprinkle over apples. Dot with margarine. Roll out remaining pastry and cover pie, pressing edges together. Make 3 slits in top crust and bake at 400° for 45 to 50 minutes. Cool before serving.

Shortcrust Pastry

If you wish, you may substitute piecrust mix, piecrust sticks, or commercially prepared pie shells in any recipe calling for this pastry.

Flour   1¾ cups
Salt   a pinch
Margarine   ½ cup
Lard* or shortening   3 tablespoons
Water   4 to 5 tablespoons

Sift flour with salt into mixing bowl. Cut in margarine and lard until mixture resembles fine bread crumbs. Add water and mix to a firm dough, then turn onto a floured board and knead lightly until smooth; do not overknead dough or it will be tough instead of flaky. Chill 15 to 20 minutes before rolling out (chilled dough is easier to roll out). Arrange dough in pie tin, fill, and bake according to directions. For a baked pie shell, line pie tin with pastry and flute edges. Line pastry with 2 layers of tissue paper larger than the pie shell. Completely fill the pie shell with dried beans and bake at 375° for 15 minutes. Remove beans by lifting out tissue paper; discard. Bake pie shell 5 minutes more; cool before filling. Makes enough for 1 8-inch double-crust pie or 2 8-inch pie shells.
Note: Liberally pierce the bottom of the pie shell before adding the filling or before baking; this ensures that steam will escape so the bottom crust will not become soggy.
* Although some people prefer shortening, I feel lard produces much better results.

Candied Apple Pie

Medium apples   7, peeled, cored, and sliced
Butter or margarine   ½ cup
Brown sugar   1 cup
Flour   1 cup

Arrange apples in a buttered 9-inch pie tin; set aside. Cream butter and brown sugar together until light and fluffy; add flour and continue beating until well blended. Cover apples with mixture and bake at 325° for 50 minutes. Cool before serving. Serves 6.

Osgood Pie

Raisins   1 cup, cooked until plump
Apples   1 cup peeled, cored, and chopped
Pecans or other nuts   1 cup chopped
Margarine   1 cup, melted
Eggs   4, beaten
Vinegar   1 tablespoon
Sugar   2 cups
Shortcrust Pastry (see Index)
   2 9-inch pie shells, unbaked

Combine first 7 ingredients and mix well. Pour ½ into each pie shell and bake at 375° for 40 minutes. Cool before serving. Makes 2 pies.

Golden Apple-Yogurt Pie

Rich Shortcrust Pastry for 9-inch double-crust pie
Apples 6, peeled, cored, and sliced
Vanilla yogurt ½ cup
Honey ½ cup
Light brown sugar ¼ cup
Nutmeg ½ teaspoon
Cinnamon 1 teaspoon

Roll out ½ of pastry and line a 9-inch pie tin; fill with apples. Thoroughly mix remaining ingredients and pour over apples. Roll out remaining pastry and lay over apples; flute edges and cut slits in top crust. Bake at 425° for 20 minutes, then reduce heat to 350° and bake 20 minutes more. Cool before serving.
Variation: Brush milk over top crust, then sprinkle with sugar before baking, for a slight glaze.

Rich Shortcrust Pastry

If you wish, you may substitute piecrust mix, piecrust sticks, or commercially prepared pie shells in any recipe calling for this pastry.

Flour 2 cups
Salt a pinch
Butter or margarine ¾ cup
Sugar 1 tablespoon
Egg yolk 1
Cold water 3 tablespoons

Sift flour with salt; cut in butter until small pieces are well coated, then rub them in, using your fingertips, until mixture resembles fine bread crumbs. Stir in sugar. Beat egg yolk and water together; add to butter mixture and mix quickly to a firm dough. Turn onto a floured board and knead lightly until smooth; do not overknead dough or it will be tough instead of flaky. Chill 15 to 20 minutes before rolling out (chilled dough is easier to roll out). Arrange dough in pie tin, fill, and bake according to directions. For a baked pie shell, line pie tin with pastry and flute edges. Line pastry with 2 layers of tissue paper larger than the pie shell. Completely fill the pie shell with dried beans and bake at 375° for 15 minutes. Remove beans by lifting out tissue paper; discard. Bake pie shell 5 minutes more; cool before filling. Makes enough for 1 9-inch double-crust pie or 2 9-inch pie shells.

Note: Liberally pierce the bottom of the unbaked pie shell before adding the filling; this ensures that steam will escape so the bottom crust will not become soggy.

No-Crust Apple Pie

Apples 5 cups peeled, cored, and in ½-inch slices
Sugar ½ cup
Nutmeg ¼ teaspoon
Cinnamon ½ teaspoon
Water ½ cup
Margarine 3 tablespoons
Brown sugar ¼ cup
Flour ½ cup, sifted
Baking powder ½ teaspoon
Salt ¼ teaspoon

In a 2-quart saucepan, toss apples with sugar, nutmeg, and cinnamon. Add water and cook over moderate heat for 10 minutes, or until apples are partially cooked. Turn into a buttered 9-inch pie tin. Cream margarine and gradually add brown sugar. Sift flour with baking powder and salt, add to creamed mixture, and mix thoroughly. Spoon over apples and bake at 350° for 45 minutes. Cool before serving. Serves 6 to 8.

Magic Crust Apple Pie

Sugar   ¾ cup
Egg   1, beaten
Flour   ½ cup
Baking powder   1 teaspoon
Nutmeg   ¼ teaspoon
Salt   ¼ teaspoon
Walnuts   ½ cup chopped
Apples   1 cup peeled, cored, and finely chopped

Beat sugar into egg and continue beating until very well blended. Sift together flour, baking powder, nutmeg, and salt; add to sugar and egg, then stir in walnuts and apples. Pour mixture into well-greased 8-inch pie tin and bake at 350° for 30 minutes. Cool before serving.

Apple Cream Pie

Sour cream   1 cup
Milk   1 cup
Instant vanilla pudding   1 3½-ounce package
Apples   1 cup peeled, cored, and chopped
Graham cracker crust   8-inch pie shell
Whipping cream   ½ cup
Sugar   2 teaspoons
Vanilla   ½ teaspoon

Mix sour cream with milk and beat until smooth, then slowly add to pudding mix. Blend in apples and stir until mixture begins to set. Pour into pie shell and chill at least 1 hour. Just before serving, whip cream until stiff, gradually adding sugar and vanilla; spread over top of pie.

Apple Custard Pie

Flour 2 tablespoons
Sugar ¼ cup
Rich Shortcrust Pastry (see Index)
    9-inch pie shell, unbaked
Apples 5, peeled, cored, and halved
Egg 1, beaten
Evaporated milk 1½ cups
Flour 2 tablespoons
Sugar ¾ cup
Nutmeg ¼ teaspoon
Cinnamon ¼ teaspoon

Sprinkle 2 tablespoons flour and ¼ cup sugar over bottom of pie shell. Arrange apples, cut sides up, in pie shell. Combine egg and evaporated milk, and pour over apples. Combine remaining ingredients; sprinkle over all. Bake at 450° for 10 minutes, then reduce temperature to 325° and cook 45 to 60 minutes more. Chill well and serve.

Sour Cream Apple Pie

Sugar ½ cup
Flour 1 tablespoon
Salt ¼ teaspoon
Egg 1, slightly beaten
Sour cream ¾ cup
Vanilla 1 teaspoon
Apples 2 cups peeled, cored, and chopped
Rich Shortcrust Pastry (see Index)
    9-inch pie shell, unbaked
Flour ¼ cup
Brown sugar ¼ cup
Butter 2 tablespoons
Cinnamon ½ teaspoon

Combine sugar, flour, and salt; add egg, sour cream, and vanilla. Mix in apples, pour mixture into pie shell, and bake at 450° for 10 minutes. Combine remaining ingredients, mixing until butter is well blended. Sprinkle over pie and bake at 350° for 25 to 30 minutes more. Cool before serving.

Cheezy Apple Pie

Apples 5 cups peeled, cored, and thinly sliced
Sugar ½ cup
Cinnamon 1 teaspoon
Shortcrust Pastry (see Index)
    8-inch pie shell, unbaked
Brown sugar ⅓ cup
Flour ½ cup
Butter or margarine ¼ cup
Cheddar cheese 1 cup grated

Combine apples, sugar, and cinnamon; arrange in pie shell. Combine brown sugar, flour, and butter, mixing with a fork until mixture resembles crumbs; sprinkle over apples. Bake at 400° for 35 minutes. Sprinkle cheese over pie and return to oven, baking just until cheese melts. Serve warm.

Apple-Ricotta Pie

Apples 4, peeled, cored, and sliced
Rich Shortcrust Pastry (see Index)
    8-inch pie shell, baked
Ricotta cheese 8 ounces
Brown sugar ½ cup
Egg 1
Plain yogurt ½ cup
Cinnamon ⅛ teaspoon
Vanilla 1 teaspoon

Arrange layers of overlapping apples in pie shell. Beat remaining ingredients together with a fork; pour over apples. Bake at 350° for 30 minutes, or until knife inserted in center comes out clean. Cool and chill in refrigerator for at least 1 hour before serving.

Strawberry-Apple Pie

Shortcrust Pastry (see Index)
    for 9-inch double-crust pie
Quick-cooking tapioca   1½ tablespoons
Salt   ½ teaspoon
Strawberries   1 cup crushed or
    Frozen strawberries   1 10-ounce package, thawed
Sugar   ½ cup
Apples   3, peeled, cored, and sliced
Lemon juice   2 teaspoons
Margarine   1 tablespoon

Roll out ½ of pastry and line a 9-inch pie tin. Combine next 6 ingredients and pour into pie shell; dot with margarine. Roll out remaining pastry and cover pie; flute edges and cut slits in top crust. Bake at 375° for 45 minutes. Cool before serving.

Apple-Mince Pie

Brown sugar   ¾ cup
Cream   ¾ cup
Salt   ¼ teaspoon
Mincemeat   1 cup
Apples   2 cups peeled, cored, and chopped
Rich Shortcrust Pastry (see Index)
    9-inch pie shell, unbaked
Walnuts   ½ cup chopped
Nutmeg   ⅛ teaspoon

Combine brown sugar, cream, and salt; mix in mincemeat and apples. Pour mixture into pie shell, sprinkle with walnuts and nutmeg, and bake at 375° for 35 to 40 minutes. Cool before serving.

Apple-Rhubarb Pie

Shortcrust Pastry (see Index)
 for 9-inch double-crust pie
Apples 2 cups peeled, cored, and sliced
Rhubarb 2 cups sliced
Sugar ¾ cup
Flour 2 tablespoons
Nutmeg ¼ teaspoon

Roll out ½ of pastry and line a 9-inch pie tin. Combine remaining ingredients and mix well; pour into pie shell. Roll out remaining pastry and cover pie; flute and seal edges, and cut 6 slits in top crust. Bake at 400° for 35 to 40 minutes. Cool before serving.

Thanksgiving Pie

Apple butter 1 cup
Canned pumpkin 1 cup
Brown sugar ½ cup
Salt ½ teaspoon
Cinnamon ¾ teaspoon
Nutmeg ¾ teaspoon
Cloves a dash
Ginger ⅛ teaspoon
Eggs 3, beaten
Half-and-half 1 cup, scalded and slightly cooled
Shortcrust Pastry (see Index)
 9-inch pie shell, unbaked

Thoroughly combine first 8 ingredients. Add eggs, then gradually add half-and-half. Pour mixture into pie shell and bake at 375° for 35 to 40 minutes. Cool before serving.

Applesauce Custard Pie

Applesauce 2 cups
Margarine ¼ cup, melted
Sugar 1 cup
Salt ½ teaspoon
Cinnamon ¼ teaspoon
Lemon juice 3 tablespoons
Lemon peel 1 teaspoon grated
Eggs 4
Shortcrust Pastry (see Index)
    10-inch pie shell, unbaked and edges fluted

Combine first 8 ingredients; mix well and pour into pie shell. Bake at 450° for 15 minutes; then reduce heat to 375° and bake 30 minutes more, or until knife inserted in center comes out clean. Cool before serving.

Applesauce Chiffon Pie

Egg yolks 2, slightly beaten
Milk 1 cup
Salt ½ teaspoon
Sugar ¼ cup
Unflavored gelatin 1 tablespoon
Water ¼ cup
Lemon peel 1 teaspoon grated
Salt ¼ teaspoon
Nutmeg ¼ teaspoon
Applesauce 2½ cups
Egg whites 2
Sugar 2 tablespoons
Rich Shortcrust Pastry (see Index)
    9-inch pie shell, baked

Cook egg yolks, milk, salt, and sugar together in top of double boiler until mixture thickens and coats the back of a spoon. Soften gelatin in water and combine with mixture in double boiler. Add lemon peel, salt, nutmeg, and applesauce; stir well. Chill mixture until nearly set. Beat egg whites with remaining sugar until stiff; fold into chilled mixture. Turn into pie shell and chill.

Glazed Apple Cookies

Flour   2 cups
Baking soda   1 teaspoon
Salt   ½ teaspoon
Cinnamon   1 teaspoon
Cloves   1 teaspoon
Nutmeg   1 teaspoon
Margarine   ½ cup
Brown sugar   1⅓ cups
Egg   1, well beaten
Apples   1 cup peeled, cored, and finely chopped
Raisins   1 cup, chopped
Nuts   1 cup chopped
Milk   ¼ cup
Glaze

Mix together flour and baking soda. Combine next 7 ingredients until very well blended. Stir in ½ of flour mixture, plus apples, raisins, and nuts. Blend in milk and remaining flour mixture; stir well. Drop by tablespoonfuls, 2 inches apart, onto greased cookie sheets. Bake at 400° for 11 minutes. Glaze cookies while still warm. Makes 3 dozen cookies.

Glaze

Powdered sugar   1½ cups
Butter   1 tablespoon, softened
Vanilla   ¼ teaspoon
Salt   ¼ teaspoon
Cream   2½ tablespoons

Blend all ingredients together.

Sugarless Apple-Date Cookies

Dates ½ pound, chopped
Water ¼ cup
Oil ⅔ cup
Apple 1, peeled, cored, and shredded
Salt ½ teaspoon
Vanilla 1 teaspoon
Rolled oats 3 cups
Cinnamon ⅛ teaspoon
Walnuts ½ cup chopped

Combine dates and water in a saucepan; cook over medium heat until soft. Beat mixture to paste with electric mixer, then beat in oil until mixture is very thick. Add apple, salt, and vanilla, then stir in oats. Allow batter to sit 10 minutes to absorb moisture, then add cinnamon and nuts. Drop by teaspoonfuls onto ungreased cookie sheets and bake at 350° for 15 to 20 minutes; watch cookies carefully because they burn easily. Makes 3 dozen cookies.

Applesauce Cookies

Sugar 1 cup
Margarine 1 cup
Egg 1
Flour 2 cups
Baking powder 1 tablespoon
Salt ½ teaspoon
Cinnamon ½ teaspoon
Cloves ¼ teaspoon
Raisins ½ cup
Nuts ½ cup chopped
Applesauce 1 cup

Cream together sugar and margarine; add egg. Mix in next 7 ingredients, then add applesauce. Drop by teaspoonfuls, 2 inches apart, onto greased cookie sheets. Bake 15 to 20 minutes at 350°. Makes 4 dozen cookies.

Apple–Peanut Butter Cookies

Flour 1¾ cups
Baking soda ½ teaspoon
Salt ½ teaspoon
Nutmeg ¼ teaspoon
Margarine ½ cup
Peanut butter ½ cup
Sugar ½ cup
Brown sugar ½ cup
Egg 1
Vanilla ½ teaspoon
Apples ½ cup peeled, cored, and shredded

Sift together flour, soda, salt, and nutmeg. Cream together margarine, peanut butter, sugar, and brown sugar; add egg, vanilla, and apple. Stir in sifted ingredients and blend thoroughly, then chill 30 minutes. Shape rounded teaspoonfuls into balls and place on greased cookie sheets; flatten dough with fork. Bake at 375° for 12 to 15 minutes. Makes 3½ dozen cookies.

Applescotch Brownies

Margarine ¼ cup
Light brown sugar 1 cup
Egg 1
Applesauce ½ cup
Flour ¾ cup
Baking powder 1 teaspoon
Salt ½ teaspoon
Vanilla ½ teaspoon
Butterscotch chips ¼ cup
Walnuts ½ cup coarsely chopped

Melt margarine in a large saucepan; remove from heat. Add brown sugar and stir until well blended; cool, then beat in egg and applesauce. Sift together flour, baking powder, and salt; add to applesauce mixture and mix well. Stir in remaining ingredients and pour into greased and floured 9 by 9-inch baking pan. Bake at 350° for 20 to 25 minutes. Makes 16 brownies.
Note: These will be quite soft when removed from oven, so cool thoroughly before cutting.

Apple Upside-Down Cake

Margarine ¼ cup
Honey ½ cup
Apples 2, peeled, cored, and in ¼-inch rings
Walnuts ½ cup coarsely chopped
Maraschino cherries ⅓ cup, halved
Nutmeg ¼ teaspoon
Cinnamon ½ teaspoon
Yellow cake mix 1 18½-ounce package,
 prepared according to directions on package

Melt margarine in a 9 by 13-inch pan. Add honey and apple rings; cook 3 minutes over medium high heat, turning once. Neatly arrange apple rings in bottom of pan, then add nuts and cherries. Add spices to cake batter, pour into pan, and bake at 350° for 30 to 35 minutes. Cool cake in pan for 5 minutes, then turn upside-down onto a serving dish. Serve warm.

Caramel Apple Upside-Down Cake

Apples 2, peeled, cored, and in ¼-inch slices
Caramels ½ pound
Apple juice ½ cup
Butter 2 tablespoons
Flour 1 cup
Baking powder 1 teaspoon
Salt ¼ teaspoon
Eggs 3
Sugar ¾ cup
Vanilla 1 teaspoon
Apple juice ⅓ cup
Whipped cream topping (optional)

Arrange apple slices in a well-greased 9 by 13-inch pan. In a saucepan, combine caramels with ½ cup apple juice, and cook over medium heat until smooth, stirring frequently. Stir in butter, then pour mixture over apples. Sift together flour, baking powder, and salt. Beat eggs until light and fluffy; gradually add sugar, then vanilla, then remaining apple juice. Fold in sifted ingredients, ⅓ at a time. Pour batter over apples and bake at 350° for 30 to 35 minutes. Cool cake, then turn out, upside down, onto serving dish; serve with whipped cream.

Red Ring Upside-Down Cake

Spiced apple rings 1 14-ounce jar
Red cinnamon candies 2 tablespoons
Red apple jelly ¼ cup
Cinnamon ½ teaspoon
Flour 1¾ cups
Baking powder 2 teaspoons
Salt ½ teaspoon
Egg whites 3
Sugar 1 cup
Margarine ½ cup
Milk ¾ cup
Almond extract ½ teaspoon

Drain apple rings, reserving ½ cup liquid. Combine cinnamon candies and reserved liquid in a 10-inch ovenproof frying pan; simmer until candies dissolve. Add jelly, stir until it melts, and set mixture aside. Sift together cinnamon, flour, baking powder, and salt. Beat egg whites until they form soft peaks; gradually add ¼ cup sugar and beat until egg whites form stiff peaks. Cream remaining sugar with margarine until light and fluffy. Alternately add dry ingredients and milk to creamed mixture, then fold in egg whites and almond extract. Arrange apple rings in frying pan; pour batter over rings. Bake at 350° for 35 to 40 minutes. Let cake cool only slightly, then invert onto a serving dish.

Dutch Apple Cake

Flour 1¼ cups
Salt ½ teaspoon
Sugar 1 teaspoon
Baking powder 1 teaspoon
Butter ½ cup
Egg yolk 1
Milk 2 tablespoons
Apples 2 cups peeled, cored, and in eighths
Brown sugar ¾ cup
Flour 1½ tablespoons
Butter 2 tablespoons
Cinnamon ¼ teaspoon
Nutmeg ¼ teaspoon

Sift together flour, salt, sugar, and baking powder; combine with butter, egg yolk, and milk. Line a buttered 8 by 8-inch cake pan with mixture; cover with apples. Combine remaining ingredients and sprinkle over apples. Bake at 375° for 30 minutes, or until apples are tender. Cool before serving.

Sue's Apple Cake

Sugar 1 cup
Apples 2 cups peeled, cored, and sliced
Cinnamon 1 teaspoon
Flour 1 cup
Salt ½ teaspoon
Baking soda ¾ teaspoon
Egg 1, beaten
Oil ½ cup
Vanilla 1 teaspoon
Walnuts ½ cup chopped (optional)

Pour sugar over apples; set aside. Sift together cinnamon, flour, salt, and baking soda, then resift and add to apples. Mix in remaining ingredients, stirring only until just mixed. Pour batter into a buttered 8 by 8-inch pan and bake at 375° for 35 minutes. Allow cake to cool before turning out and cutting.

Apple Butter Cake

Flour 2¼ cups
Baking powder 1 teaspoon
Baking soda 1 teaspoon
Salt ½ teaspoon
Nutmeg ½ teaspoon
Margarine ½ cup
Sugar 1 cup
Eggs 2
Apple butter ¾ cup
Vanilla 1 teaspoon
Sour cream 1 cup
Brown sugar ½ cup
Cinnamon 1 teaspoon
Walnuts ½ cup chopped

Sift together first 5 ingredients; set aside. Cream together margarine and sugar, then add eggs, 1 at a time. Beat in apple butter and vanilla. Alternately add sour cream and dry ingredients to apple butter mixture. Pour ½ of batter into a greased and floured 9 by 13-inch pan. Combine remaining ingredients and sprinkle ½ over batter. Cover with remaining batter and sprinkle with remaining topping. Bake at 350° for 40 to 45 minutes. Cool and serve.

Applesauce-Nut Bundt Cake

Yellow cake mix 1 18½-ounce package
Instant vanilla pudding 1 3¾-ounce package
Walnuts ½ cup chopped
Raisins ½ cup
Cinnamon 1 teaspoon
Applesauce 1½ cups
Oil ¼ cup
Eggs 3

In large bowl, mix together all ingredients until moistened, then stir vigorously for 1 minute. Pour batter into a greased and floured 10-inch bundt pan and bake at 350° for 40 to 45 minutes. Cool for 30 minutes before turning out. Serves 12.

Circus Bundt Cake

Flour 2 cups
Sugar 1⅓ cups
Baking powder 2 teaspoons
Salt 1 teaspoon
Oil ¾ cup
Crushed pineapple 1 cup drained
Vanilla 1 teaspoon
Eggs 2
Apples 1 cup peeled, cored, and finely chopped
Raisins ¾ cup
Flaked coconut ¾ cup
Walnuts ¾ cup chopped
Miniature marshmallows ¾ cup

Combine first 8 ingredients in large bowl; beat with electric mixer for 3 minutes. Stir in remaining ingredients, then pour into greased and floured 10-inch bundt pan. Bake at 325° for 75 minutes. Cool 15 minutes, then turn out to finish cooling. Leftover cake should be refrigerated.

Applesauce Fruitcake

Flour 3 cups sifted
Baking soda 2 teaspoons
Salt ¼ teaspoon
Cinnamon 2 teaspoons
Cloves 1½ teaspoons
Nuts 2 cups chopped
Raisins 2 cups
Dates 1 cup chopped
Margarine ½ cup
Brown sugar ¾ cup
Eggs 2
Applesauce 2 cups

Combine first 5 ingredients and sift. Mix nuts, raisins, and dates with 1 cup of flour mixture; set aside. Cream margarine until light and fluffy, gradually add brown sugar, and continue beating. Add eggs, 1 at a time. Add flour mixture alternately with applesauce, beating well after each addition. Stir in fruit and nut mixture, then spoon batter into 1 well-greased 8 by 11-inch loaf pan or 2 well-greased 3 by 6-inch loaf pans. Bake at 350° for 35 to 40 minutes. Cool before serving.

Pineapple-Applesauce Fruitcake

Flour 2 cups
Baking soda 2 teaspoons
Cloves ½ teaspoon
Nutmeg ½ teaspoon
Butter ½ cup
Sugar 1 cup
Egg 1, beaten
Applesauce 1½ cups
Raisins 1 cup
Nuts 1 cup coarsely chopped
Pineapple chunks 1 cup drained
Dates 1 cup diced
Vanilla 1 teaspoon

Sift together flour, baking soda, and spices; set aside. Cream together butter and sugar, add egg, and mix well. Add remaining ingredients, then carefully stir in flour mixture. Pour into an 8-inch springform pan and bake at 350° for 1 hour. Cool before serving.

Spice Cake Frosting

Brown sugar   ¾ cup
Light corn syrup   2 tablespoons
Egg white   1
Apple juice   3 tablespoons
Cinnamon   a dash
Walnuts   ⅓ cup finely chopped

Combine first 5 ingredients in top of double boiler and, over boiling water, beat rapidly until mixture stands in stiff peaks. Remove from heat and stir in walnuts. Makes enough to frost 2 9-inch layers.

October Frosting

Pumpkin pie spice   a dash
Sugar   1 cup
Apple juice   ⅓ cup
Light corn syrup   1 tablespoon
Egg whites   2
Apple   2 tablespoons grated
Yellow food coloring   2 drops
Red food coloring   1 drop

Combine first 5 ingredients in top of double boiler and beat over boiling water until mixture forms stiff peaks. Remove from heat, add apple and food colorings, and continue beating until spreading consistency is obtained. Makes enough to frost 2 9-inch layers.

Apple Fluff Frosting

Egg white 1
Sugar ¾ cup
Salt a dash
Applesauce ½ cup
Light corn syrup 1 teaspoon
Cinnamon ⅛ teaspoon

Combine all ingredients in top of a double boiler and beat for 1 minute. Place over boiling water and beat 4 minutes, or until frosting forms stiff peaks; be careful not to overcook. Remove from boiling water and beat until it reaches spreading consistency. Enough to frost 12 cupcakes.

Apple Filling

Apples 3, peeled and grated
Lemon peel of 1 lemon, grated
Sugar 1 cup
Egg 1
Lemon juice of 1 lemon

In heavy saucepan, combine apples, lemon peel, sugar, and egg; stir well. Add lemon juice, beat well, and cook mixture over moderate heat until very thick, stirring constantly. Cool before using. Makes enough to fill 1 9-inch layer cake.

Applesauce-Spice Filling

Brown sugar ⅓ cup
Flour 2 tablespoons
Nutmeg ½ teaspoon
Cinnamon ½ teaspoon
Cloves ½ teaspoon
Egg yolk 1
Applesauce 1¾ cups

Combine all ingredients and cook over medium heat for 10 to 12 minutes, or until thick, stirring constantly. Makes enough to fill 1 9-inch layer cake.

U.S. and Metric Measurements

Approximate conversion formulas are given below for commonly used U.S. and metric kitchen measurements.

Teaspoons	x	5	= milliliters
Tablespoons	x	15	= milliliters
Fluid ounces	x	30	= milliliters
Fluid ounces	x	0.03	= liters
Cups	x	240	= milliliters
Cups	x	0.24	= liters
Pints	x	0.47	= liters
Dry pints	x	0.55	= liters
Quarts	x	0.95	= liters
Dry quarts	x	1.1	= liters
Gallons	x	3.8	= liters
Ounces	x	28	= grams
Ounces	x	0.028	= kilograms
Pounds	x	454	= grams
Pounds	x	0.45	= kilograms
Milliliters	x	0.2	= teaspoons
Milliliters	x	0.07	= tablespoons
Milliliters	x	0.034	= fluid ounces
Milliliters	x	0.004	= cups
Liters	x	34	= fluid ounces
Liters	x	4.2	= cups
Liters	x	2.1	= pints
Liters	x	1.82	= dry pints
Liters	x	1.06	= quarts
Liters	x	0.91	= dry quarts
Liters	x	0.26	= gallons
Grams	x	0.035	= ounces
Grams	x	0.002	= pounds
Kilograms	x	35	= ounces
Kilograms	x	2.2	= pounds

Temperature Equivalents

Fahrenheit	− 32	× 5	÷ 9	= Celsius
Celsius	× 9	÷ 5	+ 32	= Fahrenheit

U.S. Equivalents

1 teaspoon	= ⅓ teaspoon
1 tablespoon	= 3 teaspoons
2 tablespoons	= 1 fluid ounce
4 tablespoons	= ¼ cup or 2 ounces
5⅓ tablespoons	= ⅓ cup or 2⅔ ounces
8 tablespoons	= ½ cup or 4 ounces
16 tablespoons	= 1 cup or 8 ounces
⅜ cup	= ¼ cup plus 2 tablespoons
⅝ cup	= ½ cup plus 2 tablespoons
⅞ cup	= ¾ cup plus 2 tablespoons
1 cup	= ½ pint or 8 fluid ounces
2 cups	= 1 pint or 16 fluid ounces
1 liquid quart	= 2 pints or 4 cups
1 liquid gallon	= 4 quarts

Metric Equivalents

1 milliliter	= 0.001 liter
1 liter	= 1000 milliliters
1 milligram	= 0.001 gram
1 gram	= 1000 milligrams
1 kilogram	= 1000 grams

Index

Appetizers
Chicken Liver and Apple Kabobs, 17
Deviled Dip, 16
Pomme Fondue, 16
Apple chart, 10–11

Baked Apples
Baked Apples, 62
Baked Apples with Cranberry Sauce, 63
Easy Apples, 62
Orange Apples, 63
Stuffed Meringue Apples, 64

Beverages
Hot Apple Nog, 18
Hot Spiced Cider, 17
Spiced Apple Shake, 17
Wassail, 18

Breads
Apple Bread, 30–31
Apple Butter Bread, 32
Apple-Cheddar Bread, 33
Apple Crowns, 35
Apple Gems, 36
Apple-Pumpkin Bread, 34
Applesauce Loaf, 32
Hearty Wheat Bread, 31
Johnnycake Surprise, 35
Nutty Apple Muffins, 36
Plum-Apple Loaf, 34
Z. Appleseed Bread, 33

Breakfasts
Apple Pancakes, 25
Apple Roll-Ups, 26
Breakfast Puffs, 24
German Pancake, 25
Quick Apple Roll-Ups, 26
Rise-and-Shine Cereal, 24
Sweet Rolls with Apple, 27

Brunches
Apple Blintzes, 28
Apple Brunchies, 28
Apple-Cheddar Brunch Dumplings, 27
Apple-Filled Brunch Cake, 29
Coffee Cake with Apple Streusel Topping, 30

Butter
Apple Butter, 20

Cakes
Apple Butter Cake, 98
Applesauce Fruitcake, 100
Applesauce-Nut Bundt Cake, 98
Apple Upside-Down Cake, 95
Caramel Apple Upside-Down Cake, 95
Circus Bundt Cake, 99

Dutch Apple Cake, 96–97
Pineapple-Applesauce Fruitcake, 100
Red Ring Upside-Down Cake, 96
Sue's Apple Cake, 97

Candy
Apple-Nutlettes, 80

Cereal
Rise-and-Shine Cereal, 24

Choosing apples, 8–9, 10–11

Chutney
Apple-Raisin Chutney, 21

Coffee cakes
Apple-Filled Brunch Cake, 29
Coffee Cake with Apple Streusel Topping, 30
Sweet Rolls with Apple, 27

Cookies
Applesauce Cookies, 93
Applescotch Brownies, 94
Apple–Peanut Butter Cookies, 94
Glazed Apple Cookies, 92
Sugarless Apple-Date Cookies, 93

Crepes
Apple-Cinnamon Crepes with Vanilla Sauce, 72
Dessert Crepes, 73

Crisps
Apple Peanut Crisp, 70
Apple Sesame Crisp, 70
Healthy Apple Crisp, 71

Desserts
Apple Brown Betty, 71
Apple-Cinnamon Crepes with Vanilla Sauce, 72–73
Apple Crepe Cake with Apricot Sauce, 74
Apple Dumplings, 76
Apple-Mint Mousse, 68
Apple-Nutlettes, 80
Apple Parfait, 68
Apple Peanut Crisp, 70
Apple Pudding, 66
Applesauce Soufflé, 69
Apple Sesame Crisp, 70
Apple Squares, 77
Apples Valencia, 65
Apple Tapioca, 67
Apple Tapioca Ambrosia, 67
Autumn Apple Bake, 80
Baked Apple-Graham Pudding, 66
Baked Apples, 62
Baked Apples with Cranberry Sauce, 63
Bourdelots, 75
Candied Fruit and Apple Bake, 64–65

Index

Caramel Apples, 80
Cinnamon-Apple Pinwheels, 79
Easy Apples, 62
Healthy Apple Crisp, 71
Kitchen Cobbler, 69
Lois's Apple Torten, 78
Orange Apples, 63
Rosy Dumplings, 76–77
Sour Cream Apple Squares, 78
Stuffed Meringue Apples, 64
Wonderful Rice Pudding, 66–67
Drying apples, 12–13
Dumplings
Apple-Cheddar Brunch Dumplings, 27
Apple Dumplings, 76
Rosy Dumplings, 76–77

Fillings
Apple Filling, 102
Applesauce-Spice Filling, 102
Freezing apples, 9, 12
Frostings
Apple Fluff Frosting, 102
October Frosting, 101
Spice Cake Frosting, 101

Growing apples, 8

History of apples, 7–8

Jam and jelly
Apple Jelly, 19
Pear and Apple Jam, 19

Main dishes
Beef
 Apple and Beef Ragout, 50
 Liver and Apples, 51
 Meat Loaf with Apples, 50
Chicken
 Baked Chicken with Apples, 58
 Sweet-and-Sour Chicken, 59
Lamb
 Lamb and Apple Stew with Biscuits, 57
Pork
 Apple-Stuffed Crown Roast of Pork, 52–53
 Apple–Sweet Potato Casserole with Sausages, 56
 Frankfurter-Apple Bake, 57
 Ham-Apple Casserole, 55
 Pork Chop Stew, 55
 Pork Chops with Apple Rings, 54
 Sausages and Apples, 56
 Smothered Pork Chops, 54
 Stuffed Pork Chops, 53
Veal
 Stuffed Veal Birds, 52

Measurements, U.S. and metric, 103–4
Muffins
Apple Crowns, 35
Apple Gems, 36
Nutty Apple Muffins, 36

Pancakes
Apple Pancakes, 25
German Pancake, 25
Pastry (piecrusts)
Rich Shortcrust Pastry, 84–85
Shortcrust Pastry, 82
Pies
Apple Cream Pie, 86
Apple Custard Pie, 87
Apple-Mince Pie, 89
Apple Pie, 82
Apple-Rhubarb Pie, 90
Apple-Ricotta Pie, 88
Applesauce Chiffon Pie, 91
Applesauce Custard Pie, 91
Candied Apple Pie, 83
Cheezy Apple Pie, 88
Golden Apple-Yogurt Pie, 84–85
Magic Crust Apple Pie, 86
No-Crust Apple Pie, 85
Osgood Pie, 83
Sour Cream Apple Pie, 87
Strawberry-Apple Pie, 89
Thanksgiving Pie, 90
Preserves
Apple Butter, 20
Apple Jelly, 19
Apple-Raisin Chutney, 21
Apple Relish, 20
Pear and Apple Jam, 19
Puddings
Apple Pudding, 66
Apple Tapioca, 67
Apple Tapioca Ambrosia, 67
Baked Apple-Graham Pudding, 66
Wonderful Rice Pudding, 66–67

Relish
Apple Relish, 20

Salads
American Apple Salad, 39
Apple-Sauerkraut Salad, 40
Christmas Salad, 40
Curried Chicken Salad, 41
Ginger Ale Salad, 42
Ham and Apple Slaw, 40
Marinated Mushroom Salad, 39
Molded Apple-Cheese Salad, 42
Molded Apple Cream, 43
Scandinavian Shrimp Salad, 41
Waldorf Salad, 38

Sandwiches
　Creamy Herring Sandwiches, 38
　Delicious Chicken Sandwiches, 38
Sauces
　Applesauce, 21
　Apricot Sauce, 74
　Cinnamon-Cider Sauce, 22
　Spiced Pineapple-Raisin-Cider Sauce, 22
　Sugarless Applesauce, 22
　Vanilla Sauce, 73
Side dishes
　Apple Stir Fry, 45
　Baked Apple Relish Cups, 46
　Fried Apples, 45
　Glazed Apple Bake, 46
　Minted Apples, 44
　Noodles and Apples, 47
　Poached Apples, 44
　Red Cabbage Casserole, 47
　Spiced Apples, 43
Storing apples, 9, 12–13
Stuffings
　Apple and Raisin Stuffing, 48
　Apple-Prune Stuffing, 48
Toppings
　Apple Topping, 25

U.S. and metric measurements, 103–4

Varieties of apples, 10–11

Other Books from Pacific Search Press

Asparagus: The Sparrowgrass Cookbook by Autumn Stanley
The Birdhouse Book: Building Houses, Feeders, and Baths by Don McNeil
Bone Appétit! Natural Foods for Pets
　　by Frances Sheridan Goulart
Border Boating: Twelve Cruises through the San Juan and
　　Gulf Islands by Phyllis and Bill Bultmann
Butterflies Afield in the Pacific Northwest
　　by William Neill/Douglas Hepburn, photography
The Carrot Cookbook by Ann Saling
Cascade Companion by Susan Schwartz/Bob and
　　Ira Spring, photography
Common Seaweeds of the Pacific Coast by J. Robert Waaland
The Crawfish Cookbook by Norma S. Upson
Cross-Country Downhill and Other Nordic Mountain Skiing
　　Techniques by Steve Barnett
The Dogfish Cookbook by Russ Mohney
The Eggplant Cookbook by Norma S. Upson
The Ferry Story by Terry Lawhead/illustrated by Paula Richards
Fire and Ice: The Cascade Volcanoes by Stephen L. Harris
The Getaway Guide: Short Vacations in the Pacific Northwest
　　by Marni and Jake Rankin
The Green Tomato Cookbook by Paula Simmons
The Handspinner's Guide to Selling by Paula Simmons
Little Mammals of the Pacific Northwest by Ellen B. Kritzman
Living Shores of the Pacific Northwest
　　by Lynwood Smith/Bernard Nist, photography
Make It and Take It: Homemade Gear for Camp and Trail
　　by Russ Mohney
Marine Mammals of Eastern North Pacific and Arctic Waters
　　edited by Delphine Haley
Messages from the Shore by Victor B. Scheffer
Minnie Rose Lovgreen's Recipe for Raising Chickens
　　by Minnie Rose Lovgreen
Mushrooms 'n Bean Sprouts: A First Step for Would-be
　　Vegetarians by Norma M. MacRae, R.D.
My Secret Cookbook by Paula Simmons
Rhubarb Renaissance: A Cookbook by Ann Saling
The Salmon Cookbook by Jerry Dennon
Sleek & Savage: North America's Weasel Family
　　by Delphine Haley
Spinning and Weaving with Wool by Paula Simmons
Starchild & Holahan's Seafood Cookbook by Adam Starchild
　　and James Holahan
The Whole Grain Bake Book by Gail L. Worstman
Why Wild Edibles? The Joys of Finding, Fixing, and Tasting
　　by Russ Mohney
Wild Mushroom Recipes by Puget Sound Mycological Society
Wild Shrubs: Finding and Growing Your Own by Joy Spurr
The Zucchini Cookbook by Paula Simmons